The 60-Day AI Advantage

How Small Businesses Crush Competitors with Risk-Free AI in a Flash

Ryan Harper

Rivanna Heights Media

Also by Rivanna Heights Media

Epic Historical Mysteries by Logan Cross
AI-Proof Your Career by Ryan Harper
Conspiracy Theories Unveiled by Logan Cross
Pickleball Made Simple by Blake Foster
The Complete Beginner's Guide To ChatGPT by Ryan Harper
Cryptocurrency Investing 101 by Jordan Taylor

CONTENTS

Claim Your Free Supplement: AI Tools for Small Businesses!

As a thank you for purchasing this book, I'm offering a special bonus: a free supplement that lists beginner-friendly AI tools to transform your business with the SHADOW Framework.

Inside this supplement, you'll find:

- **Customer Experience Boosters**: AI tools to streamline support and delight customers.
- **Operations Savers**: AI solutions to automate tasks and save time.
- **Marketing Game-Changers**: AI-driven tools for smarter campaigns and growth.
- **Financial Insights**: AI analytics to predict cash flow and optimize budgets.

Get your free supplement now by clicking or scanning the QR code:

The Competitive Clock is Ticking

You wake up at 3 AM with that familiar knot in your stomach. Not because of financial problems or staffing issues—your business is doing well. The anxiety comes from something more insidious: the nagging certainty that while you sleep, the business landscape is shifting beneath your feet.

Artificial intelligence isn't coming to transform your industry. It's already here, already being deployed, already creating winners and losers. And right now, you're not sure which side of that equation you're on.

If you're like most small business owners, you've been watching the AI revolution with a mixture of excitement and terror. You've attended webinars, bookmarked articles, and subscribed to newsletters. You understand that AI could transform your operations, but you're paralyzed by the complexity, overwhelmed by the options, and terrified of making expensive mistakes.

Meanwhile, the competitive clock keeps ticking.

The Hidden Revolution Already Underway

Here's what's happening while you research: your smartest competitors have stopped debating whether to implement AI and started figuring out how. They're not announcing their moves on LinkedIn or bragging about their technological sophistication. They're quietly testing systems, optimizing processes, and building advantages that compound every day you delay.

This isn't speculation. Across every industry, early AI adopters are capturing disproportionate benefits that grow larger over time. They're processing customer inquiries faster, identifying opportunities others miss, and reducing operational costs by thousands of dollars monthly. Most importantly, they're learning—developing expertise and intuition that will accelerate their next AI implementation while you're still planning your first.

The harsh reality is that artificial intelligence rewards businesses that start before they're ready and punishes those who wait for perfect conditions. In rapidly evolving markets, the careful planning that traditional business wisdom recommends has become a competitive liability.

Why Smart Business Owners Stay Stuck

The irony is painful: the same qualities that made you successful in building your business—careful analysis, risk management, and thorough preparation—are now keeping you from the next level of success. You're experiencing what I call "AI implementation paralysis," and you're not alone.

This paralysis manifests in predictable patterns. You've developed research addiction, consuming endless content about AI capabilities without taking action. You're suffering from perfect solution syndrome, waiting for the AI tool that addresses all your needs without limitations. You're amplifying risks while minimizing opportunities, imagining catastrophic failures while discounting potential benefits.

But here's what you need to understand: these fears aren't character flaws or signs of weakness. They're rational responses to technological uncertainty. The problem isn't that you have these concerns—it's that you're letting them prevent action while your competitors gain ground daily.

The businesses dominating the AI revolution aren't fearless or reckless. They've simply discovered that speed beats perfection in rapidly changing markets, and they've developed methodologies that eliminate most implementation risks while maximizing learning opportunities.

The Fatal Flaw in Traditional Business Wisdom

Everything you learned about business strategy assumed stable technologies and predictable timelines. "Measure twice, cut once" works perfectly when you're building a deck, but it fails catastrophically when you're trying to compete in markets where the tools evolve monthly and customer expectations shift weekly.

The traditional approach of thorough research, comprehensive planning, and careful implementation becomes dangerous when applied to AI adoption. While you're creating detailed vendor comparisons, early adopters are already optimizing their second-generation implementations. While you're waiting for proven ROI data, they're generating it through real-world operations.

The mathematics of AI adoption reveal a sobering truth: the longer you wait to implement, the harder and more expensive it becomes. Early adopters face simpler integration challenges, encounter fewer workflow disruptions, and build internal expertise that accelerates future innovations. Late adopters face steeper learning curves, higher costs, and teams that view AI as a disruptive threat rather than a competitive opportunity.

Most critically, AI advantages compound over time. Each successful implementation makes the next one easier, faster, and more profitable. Early adopters create what economists call "increasing returns to scale"—momentum that becomes increasingly difficult for competitors to match.

The Revolutionary Solution: Shadow Implementation

The path forward isn't to abandon planning altogether or to blindly implement the first AI tool you discover. The solution is to embrace a revolutionary methodology that eliminates the traditional barriers keeping you stuck in analysis mode while providing the data and confidence needed for intelligent decisions.

I call this approach "Shadow Implementation," and it's specifically designed for resource-conscious small businesses that can't afford expensive mistakes but can't afford to wait for perfect certainty either.

Shadow Implementation works by running AI solutions parallel to your existing processes. While your current systems continue operating normally, AI systems process the same inputs and generate outputs that you can compare, analyze, and optimize. You gain real-world performance data without operational risk, financial exposure, or team disruption.

This methodology transforms AI implementation from a leap of faith into a systematic validation process. Instead of choosing between paralysis and recklessness, you create a third option: informed experimentation that proves value before requiring commitment.

Your 60-Day Transformation Journey

This book will guide you through the complete journey from AI paralysis to AI mastery using the proven SHADOW Framework—a six-step methodology that hundreds of small businesses have used to implement profitable AI solutions in 60 days or less:

Screen: Identify your highest-impact AI opportunity through systematic evaluation of your business processes and ROI potential.

Harvest: Gather the essential data, resources, and stakeholder support needed for successful implementation without disrupting current operations.

Acquire: Select and configure the optimal AI solution that aligns with your specific business needs and technical capabilities.

Deploy: Launch your AI system in parallel with existing operations for safe testing and comprehensive validation.

Optimize: Refine performance based on real-world data while creating compelling documentation of ROI and business benefits.

Weave: Integrate proven AI solutions into full operations while maintaining business continuity and sustained performance.

Each step builds upon the previous one, reducing risk while increasing confidence and capability. This isn't just theory—it's a battle-tested approach that transforms AI implementation from a complex technical project into a manageable business process.

The Three-Part Transformation

Your journey through this book follows a carefully designed progression:

Part I: Awakening will shatter the illusions keeping you paralyzed. You'll discover the real cost of waiting while competitors act, understand why your implementation fears are both normal and addressable, and embrace the truth that starting before you're ready is the key to AI success. Most importantly, you'll understand exactly how Shadow Implementation eliminates the risks that have been keeping you stuck.

Part II: Implementation provides step-by-step guidance through the complete SHADOW Framework. You'll learn to identify golden opportunities, gather success resources, choose optimal solutions, deploy parallel systems, optimize performance, and integrate proven AI into your operations. Each chapter includes practical tools, real-world examples, and detailed instructions for non-technical business owners.

Part III: Acceleration shows you how to leverage your first AI success into sustained competitive advantage. You'll discover how to scale implementations across your business, revolutionize customer experiences, create self-running operations, compete with Fortune 500 marketing capabilities, gain crystal ball financial insights, and establish yourself as the AI leader in your industry.

The Choice That Defines Your Future

You're standing at a crossroads that will define your business trajectory for the next decade. One path leads to continued analysis, endless planning, and watching competitors gain advantages while you prepare. The other path leads to rapid implementation, competitive advantage, and positioning your business as an industry innovator.

The choice seems obvious, but it requires abandoning the comfortable illusion that perfect preparation prevents poor performance. In the AI revolution, perfect preparation guarantees poor performance because it delays action beyond the point of competitive relevance.

Your competitors are making this choice right now. Some are choosing the path of continued analysis, convincing themselves that more research will lead to better decisions. Others are choosing the path of informed action, implementing AI solutions that will compound their advantages over time.

The question isn't whether you'll eventually implement AI—it's whether you'll lead the transformation or be forced to follow it.

Your Awakening Begins Now

The competitive clock isn't just ticking—it's accelerating. But here's what most business owners don't realize: you still have time to catch up and even surpass early adopters if you understand what's really happening and why speed matters more than perfection.

This book will show you exactly how to do that. You'll develop not just the tactical skills for AI implementation, but the strategic mindset that separates AI leaders from AI followers. You'll learn to view uncertainty as competitive advantage, embrace implementation challenges as learning opportunities, and build the confidence that comes from proven success.

Every day you delay implementation is a day your competitors gain ground. But every day you move forward with the SHADOW Framework is a day you build advantages that become harder for others to replicate.

Your AI awakening begins with the next page, where you'll discover the reality of what's happening in your industry while you've been researching and planning. The revolution isn't coming—it's already here. But with the right approach, you can turn the threat into your greatest opportunity.

The businesses that will dominate the next decade aren't the ones with the most comprehensive AI strategies—they're the ones that start implementing AI solutions while their competitors are still planning.

Your transformation starts now.

Part I: Awakening

Rivanna Heights Media

Chapter One

The Competitor Nightmare is Real

While you've been researching AI tools, your competitors started implementing them.

That restless feeling keeping you awake at 3 AM isn't paranoia—it's your business instincts screaming a warning. Right now, as you read these words, businesses in your industry are quietly deploying AI solutions that will make their operations faster, smarter, and more profitable than yours. They're not waiting for perfect conditions, extensive training, or complete certainty about their choices.

They're simply starting.

This isn't a distant future scenario or a theoretical possibility. The competitor nightmare you've been worried about is happening right now, and every day you delay action makes their advantages harder to overcome. But here's what most business owners don't realize: you still have time to catch up and even surpass them—if you understand what's really happening and why speed matters more than perfection.

The Hidden AI Revolution in Your Backyard

You probably think you'd know if your competitors were using AI. After all, wouldn't they be bragging about it? Wouldn't there be obvious signs of their technological superiority? The uncomfortable truth is that the smartest businesses keep their AI implementations quiet. They're not announcing their competitive advantages—they're too busy capitalizing on them.

Consider Sarah, who runs a regional accounting firm with nine employees. While her competitors spent months debating which AI bookkeeping platform to choose, Sarah quietly implemented an AI-powered invoice processing system in three weeks. She didn't announce it with fanfare or post about it on LinkedIn. She simply started using it.

The results spoke for themselves:

- Invoice processing time dropped from 45 minutes to 17 minutes per client
- Error rates decreased by 39% in the first month
- Client satisfaction scores increased as reports became more accurate and timely
- Her team could handle 20% more clients without hiring additional staff

Here's the part that should terrify her competitors: Sarah gained these advantages while they were still comparing feature lists and reading reviews. By the time they finally chose their AI solution, Sarah had already optimized her system, trained her team, and captured market share from businesses that couldn't keep up with her efficiency.

This scenario plays out every day across industries. While you research, someone else implements. While you plan, someone else profits. While you wait for certainty, someone else captures the advantages that could have been yours.

The Research Trap That's Costing You Customers

Here's a painful truth most business owners refuse to face: **extensive research has become the enemy of progress**. Don't misunderstand—due diligence matters. But when research becomes an excuse for inaction, it transforms from a business tool into a competitive liability.

The average small business owner spends 4.7 months researching AI solutions before making their first implementation attempt. During those same months, early adopters in their industry complete entire AI deployments, optimize their systems, and begin capturing the benefits that research-focused competitors are still reading about.

Why does this happen? Because our business education taught us that thorough preparation prevents poor performance. In stable markets with predictable technologies, this wisdom held true. But AI isn't stable or predictable—it's rapidly evolving with new tools, features, and capabilities emerging monthly.

Consider these market realities:

Traditional Business Approach	AI Era Reality
Research thoroughly, then implement	Implement quickly, then optimize
Minimize risk through extensive planning	Minimize risk through rapid testing
Choose the "best" solution upfront	Start with "good enough" and improve
Wait for proven ROI before investing	Test small to prove ROI quickly

The businesses winning in the AI revolution understand that **perfect information doesn't exist in rapidly changing markets**. They've replaced the goal of making perfect decisions with the strategy of making fast, reversible decisions that generate real-world data.

Marcus runs a small manufacturing company that produces custom furniture. He spent six weeks researching AI inventory management systems, creating detailed comparison spreadsheets and calling references. During those same six weeks, his main competitor implemented a basic AI demand forecasting tool, discovered it reduced their raw material waste by 23%, and used the cost savings to lower their prices by 8%.

By the time Marcus finished his research and made his "perfect" choice, his competitor had already captured three new clients with their new competitive pricing. Marcus's extensive research delivered the optimal solution—but it delivered it too late to matter.

The Compound Effect of Early AI Adoption

The most dangerous aspect of delayed AI implementation isn't just missing immediate benefits—it's falling behind the compound advantages that early adopters accumulate over time. These advantages don't add linearly; they multiply, creating gaps that become increasingly difficult to close.

First-Mover Learning Curves

When businesses implement AI solutions early, they begin climbing learning curves that their competitors haven't even started. This learning isn't just technical—it's strategic, operational, and cultural.

Take Lisa, who owns a digital marketing agency with eight team members. She implemented AI content creation tools six months before her main competitors. Here's what happened during those six months:

Months 1-2: Lisa's team learned the AI tools' capabilities and limitations through daily use

Months 3-4: They developed custom workflows that integrated AI seamlessly with their existing processes

Months 5-6: They created proprietary prompts and techniques that produced consistently better results than standard approaches

When her competitors finally implemented similar AI tools, they faced the same learning curve Lisa had already completed. But Lisa didn't stop there. She used her head start to experiment with more advanced AI applications while her competitors were still mastering the basics.

The result? Lisa's agency now delivers content 60% faster than competitors while maintaining higher quality standards. Her team has become so efficient that they can take on larger projects at competitive prices, or maintain their pricing while delivering exceptional profit margins.

Data Advantage Accumulation

AI systems improve with use and data. Early implementers feed their AI tools more data, faster, which means their systems become more accurate and valuable over time. Late adopters start with systems that may be technically equivalent, but they lack the refined data models that early adopters have developed.

Consider a customer service scenario. An early AI adopter has been feeding their chatbot real customer interactions for six months. Their system now handles 78% of customer inquiries without human intervention, and it understands the nuances of their specific industry and customer base.

A late adopter implementing the same chatbot technology starts with a generic system that can only handle basic inquiries. Even if they use identical software, they're months behind in data sophistication—and their customers notice the difference in service quality.

Market Positioning Benefits

Early AI adopters don't just improve their operations—they reshape customer expectations in their favor. When you're the first business in your market to offer AI-enhanced services, you define what customers should expect from your industry.

Dr. Jennifer Martinez runs a small dental practice that implemented AI appointment scheduling and patient communication tools eight months ago. Her patients now expect instant appointment confirmations, proactive reminder systems, and personalized treatment recommendations. When they visit other dental offices, the traditional appointment systems feel outdated and inconvenient.

Jennifer didn't just improve her practice—she raised the bar for her entire local market. Competitors now must implement similar systems not to gain advantages, but simply to meet the new baseline expectations Jennifer established.

Why Analysis Paralysis Has Become a Competitive Death Sentence

The traditional business wisdom of "measure twice, cut once" assumes that thorough analysis leads to better decisions. In stable markets with well-understood technologies, this approach works. But AI markets change so rapidly that extensive analysis often produces outdated conclusions by the time you're ready to act.

The Information Decay Problem

AI vendor capabilities, pricing models, and integration options change monthly. The research you conducted three months ago may be completely irrelevant today. By the time you finish extensive analysis, the competitive landscape has shifted, new solutions have emerged, and early adopters have gained advantages that make your "perfect" choice less valuable.

David spent four months researching AI accounting software for his consulting firm. He created detailed vendor comparisons, tested free trials, and interviewed references. His final choice was technically superior to the solution his competitor implemented in week two of David's research process.

But here's what David's analysis couldn't account for: while he researched, his competitor gained four months of operational efficiency, improved client satisfaction, and additional revenue from their enhanced capacity. Even with a "better" technical solution, David started his AI journey four months behind his competitor's learning curve and market advantages.

The Perfect Solution Illusion

Many business owners delay AI implementation because they're searching for the "perfect" solution that addresses all their needs without limitations or compromises. This search for perfection creates an illusion that prevents action and ignores a fundamental truth about AI adoption: **the best solution is the one you're actually using**.

A mediocre AI tool that's been optimized through six months of real-world use will outperform a technically superior tool that you implement next quarter. The value comes not from the tool itself, but from the learning, optimization, and workflow integration that happen through consistent use.

The Certainty Trap

Business owners often wait for certainty about ROI before implementing AI solutions. They want guarantees that their investment will pay off, their team will adopt the new tools, and their operations will improve. This desire for certainty feels responsible, but it ignores the reality that **certainty only comes through experience, not analysis**.

You can't think your way to AI certainty—you have to implement your way there. Every day you wait for more certainty is another day your competitors gain real-world experience that increases their certainty while decreasing yours.

The Exponential Advantage Gap

The gap between early AI adopters and late implementers doesn't grow linearly—it compounds exponentially. This happens because AI advantages build upon themselves, creating multiple layers of competitive benefits that become increasingly difficult to overcome.

Operational Efficiency Compounds

An AI-enhanced business doesn't just work faster—it frees up human resources to focus on higher-value activities. These freed resources create additional opportunities for improvement, growth, and innovation that non-AI competitors can't match.

When Sarah's accounting firm reduced invoice processing time by 85%, her team didn't just handle existing work faster. They used their newfound time to develop new service offerings, improve client relationships, and explore additional AI applications. Each efficiency gain created capacity for further improvements, while her competitors remained stuck in manual processes.

Learning Velocity Accelerates

Businesses using AI tools learn about AI applications faster than businesses that haven't started. They develop intuition about what works, what doesn't, and where opportunities exist. This accelerated learning creates a knowledge gap that widens over time.

Lisa's marketing agency didn't just implement AI content tools—they discovered applications their competitors haven't even considered. They learned to use AI for client research, campaign optimization, and strategic planning. Their AI fluency allows them to spot new opportunities and implement solutions while competitors are still figuring out basic applications.

Market Perception Shifts

Early AI adopters often become known as the "innovative" or "cutting-edge" businesses in their markets. This reputation attracts customers who value progress and efficiency, creating a customer base that's more receptive to future innovations.

Dr. Martinez's dental practice now attracts patients specifically because of their AI-enhanced experience. These patients expect and appreciate technological sophistication, making them ideal customers for future AI implementations. Meanwhile, traditional practices compete for patients who may resist technological changes.

The Point of No Return

There's a moment in every market when AI adoption shifts from advantage to necessity. Early adopters gain competitive benefits, but late adopters face competitive survival requirements. The businesses that wait too long don't just miss advantages—they risk irrelevance.

When AI Becomes Table Stakes

In some industries, this shift has already happened. Real estate agents without AI-powered market analysis tools struggle to compete with agents who can provide instant, data-driven property valuations. Restaurants without AI inventory management face higher costs than competitors who optimize their purchasing through predictive algorithms.

The warning signs are clear: when customers begin expecting AI-enhanced services, when competitors consistently outperform you on efficiency metrics, when new market entrants launch with AI-first business models. By the time these signals become obvious, the window for gaining competitive advantages has closed.

The Recovery Challenge

Businesses that fall significantly behind in AI adoption face a recovery challenge that goes beyond just implementing technology. They must overcome the compound advantages their competitors have accumulated while simultaneously building their own AI capabilities.

This dual challenge requires more resources, creates more risk, and delivers smaller relative benefits than early implementation would have provided. The businesses that wait too long often find themselves perpetually behind, implementing yesterday's solutions while competitors explore tomorrow's possibilities.

Your Competitive Response Window

The good news is that in most industries, the competitive response window remains open. Early adopters have gained advantages, but decisive action can still capture significant benefits and prevent further competitive erosion.

Assessing Your Position

Look at your industry through this lens: Are your competitors offering services you can't match? Are they responding to customer inquiries faster than your team? Are they delivering better results with similar resources? These signals indicate AI-powered advantages that you need to address quickly.

The goal isn't to match what competitors implemented months ago—it's to leapfrog their current capabilities by learning from their experience and implementing more advanced solutions.

The Fast-Follower Advantage

Businesses that implement AI solutions after early adopters can benefit from the pioneers' learning without experiencing their mistakes. You can see which applications work, which vendors deliver results, and which approaches fail. This intelligence allows you to move faster and more confidently than the original early adopters could.

But this advantage only exists if you act quickly. The longer you wait, the more advantages early adopters accumulate, and the smaller your fast-follower benefits become.

Breaking Free from the Research Prison

The competitor nightmare is real, but it's not inevitable. You can break free from the research trap that's keeping you behind by shifting your approach from seeking perfect information to generating real experience.

The Implementation Mindset

Replace the question "What's the best AI solution?" with "What's the fastest way to start gaining AI experience?" Stop asking "How can I guarantee this will work?" and start asking "How can I test this with minimal risk?"

The businesses winning the AI race aren't the ones who made perfect choices—they're the ones who made fast choices and optimized them through experience. They understand that in rapidly changing markets, adaptability matters more than initial accuracy.

Your Competitive Recovery Plan

Your competitors have head starts, but they don't have your unique business advantages, customer relationships, or market insights. You can use these strengths to implement AI solutions that fit your specific situation better than generic approaches your competitors may have chosen.

The key is to start now, learn quickly, and use your distinctive business knowledge to guide your AI implementation strategy. Every day you delay is another day your competitors build advantages that could have been yours.

The competitor nightmare that's been keeping you awake isn't a future threat—it's a current reality. But nightmares end when you wake up and take action. Your competitors started while you researched, but you can still catch up and surpass them by starting today.

The next chapter will show you exactly why the fears that have been paralyzing you are not only normal but completely addressable through the right approach. Understanding your competition is the first step; understanding your own psychological barriers is the second step toward AI implementation success.

Chapter Two

Why Smart Business Owners Are Paralyzed

Your brain treats AI decisions like life-threatening emergencies. When you sit down to research artificial intelligence solutions for your business, your amygdala—the brain's ancient alarm system—screams danger signals as if you're facing a saber-toothed tiger. This isn't weakness or incompetence; it's human biology responding to perceived threats in exactly the way evolution designed. The same survival instincts that kept your ancestors alive now sabotage your business decisions, turning rational entrepreneurs into anxious procrastinators who research endlessly but never act.

The irony cuts deep—the very intelligence that made you successful now works against you.

The Neuroscience Behind Your AI Paralysis

Your brain processes AI implementation decisions through three distinct fear circuits, each one designed to protect you from different types of danger. Understanding these circuits is the first step toward overcoming them.

The Overwhelm Circuit fires when you encounter too many variables at once. AI presents an almost infinite array of options: machine learning, natural language processing, computer vision, chatbots, predictive analytics, automation tools, and hundreds of vendors claiming to solve problems you didn't know you had. Your prefrontal cortex—responsible for executive decision-making—simply shuts down when faced with this complexity.

Think about the last time you tried to choose an AI tool. You probably opened fifteen browser tabs, bookmarked twenty articles, and started three different comparison spreadsheets. Within an hour, you felt mentally exhausted despite making zero progress. That's your overwhelm circuit protecting you from cognitive overload by triggering the familiar response of analysis paralysis.

The Loss Aversion Circuit magnifies potential downsides while minimizing potential gains. Behavioral economists have proven that humans feel losses roughly twice as intensely as equivalent gains. When you consider investing $10,000 in AI software, your brain doesn't calculate potential benefits—it imagines that money disappearing into a technological black hole.

This circuit explains why you can easily justify spending $50,000 on a delivery truck you can see and touch, but agonize over a $5,000 AI solution that could save you $100,000 annually. The truck feels safe because it's familiar. The AI feels dangerous because it's new.

The Competence Threat Circuit triggers when your expertise feels challenged. You've built your business through deep knowledge in your field. You know your customers, understand your operations, and can solve problems others can't. AI represents a domain where your hard-earned expertise provides no advantage—where you're a beginner again.

This circuit whispers poisonous questions: "What if my employees know more about this than I do? What if I make decisions that reveal my ignorance? What if my lack of technical knowledge leads to catastrophic mistakes?" The fear of appearing incompetent often overwhelms the potential for gaining competence.

Why Investment Terror Feels So Real

The financial anxiety you experience around AI investments isn't just about money—it's about survival, identity, and control. Your business represents more than income; it's your security, your family's future, and your professional identity wrapped into one entity. When AI vendors talk about "disruption" and "transformation," your nervous system hears "threat to everything you've built."

The Sunk Cost Spiral begins before you even start. You know that AI implementation rarely stops with one tool or one process. Every vendor presentation includes phrases like "additional modules," "premium features," and "expanded capabilities." Your brain calculates not just the initial investment, but the inevitable cascade of additional expenses: training costs, integration fees, ongoing subscriptions, technical support, and consultant bills.

You've seen other business owners get trapped in technology spending spirals—starting with simple software purchases that balloon into six-figure commitments. The fear of becoming another cautionary tale about small businesses bankrupted by technology investments creates a paralysis that feels protective but actually increases your competitive vulnerability.

The Complexity Tax multiplies your financial fears. Every AI solution seems to require complementary investments: upgraded hardware, new software integrations, staff training, security enhancements, and backup systems. What looks like a $500-per-month AI tool quickly becomes a $5,000-per-month ecosystem of dependencies.

You're not wrong to worry about these costs—they're real. But your fear-based calculations often ignore the cost of inaction: lost customers, missed opportunities, and competitive disadvantages that compound daily while you remain stuck in research mode.

The Technical Helplessness Trap emerges from the gap between AI marketing promises and implementation realities. Vendors show polished demos where AI seamlessly integrates with existing systems, instantly improves performance, and requires minimal oversight. Then reality hits: APIs don't connect properly, data formats clash, workflows break, and you're completely dependent on technical support that may or may not understand your business.

This dependency feels especially threatening because it challenges your self-reliance. You've built your business by learning what you need to know and solving problems as they arise. AI introduces a level of technical complexity that resists traditional problem-solving approaches, creating a sense of helplessness that triggers deep anxiety.

The Traditional Business Wisdom Trap

The planning methodologies that made you successful in stable environments become liabilities in rapidly changing AI markets. Traditional business wisdom emphasizes careful analysis, risk mitigation, and informed decision-making—all excellent principles that backfire spectacularly in AI adoption.

The Perfect Information Fallacy suggests that better research leads to better decisions. In stable markets, this works well. If you're buying a delivery truck, you can research models, compare prices, read reviews, and make an informed choice knowing that truck technology changes slowly.

AI markets operate by different rules. The information you gather today becomes partially obsolete within months. The vendor comparison chart you spent weeks creating loses relevance as companies pivot strategies, release new features, or get acquired by competitors. The "perfect" solution you identified through extensive research may no longer exist by the time you're ready to buy.

Meanwhile, businesses that started with "good enough" solutions six months ago have learned through experience, optimized their processes, and gained competitive advantages that research alone cannot provide.

The Risk Mitigation Paradox reveals how traditional safety measures increase AI adoption risks. Conservative business wisdom suggests starting with pilot programs, extensive testing, gradual rollouts, and comprehensive backup plans. These approaches feel safe but actually increase your chances of failure.

AI tools improve through usage and data accumulation. Solutions that appear mediocre during limited testing often excel once they process real business data at scale. Conversely, AI systems that perform well in controlled pilot environments sometimes struggle with the complexity and variability of full-scale operations.

The businesses winning with AI aren't necessarily choosing better tools—they're choosing faster learning cycles. They start with imperfect solutions, gather real performance data quickly, and optimize based on actual results rather than theoretical projections.

The Consensus Requirement becomes a competitive disadvantage in fast-moving markets. Traditional business decisions benefit from stakeholder input, committee review, and consensus building. These processes ensure buy-in and reduce implementation resistance while also slowing decision-making to a crawl.

AI adoption rewards speed over consensus. By the time you've scheduled meetings, gathered opinions, addressed concerns, and achieved agreement, your competitors have implemented, tested, and optimized their solutions. The competitive advantage goes to businesses that can make AI decisions quickly and course-correct rapidly, not to those that make perfect decisions slowly.

The Psychology of Technical Inadequacy

Your relationship with AI is complicated by the gap between your business expertise and technical requirements. You're accustomed to being the expert, the problem-solver, the person others turn to for answers. AI forces you into unfamiliar territory where your hard-earned expertise provides limited advantage.

Impostor Syndrome in AI manifests as the fear that your lack of technical knowledge will be exposed at the worst possible moment. You worry about being manipulated by vendors who speak in technical jargon you don't fully understand. You fear making commitments based on incomplete understanding, then having to explain failures to employees, customers, or investors.

This fear isn't entirely irrational. The AI industry is filled with misleading marketing claims, over-promised capabilities, and solutions that work beautifully in demonstrations but fail in real-world applications. Your caution protects you from obvious scams while also protecting you from legitimate opportunities.

The Competence Cliff describes the sudden drop from feeling knowledgeable to feeling ignorant when AI topics arise. In your industry, you can evaluate quality, assess value, and make confident decisions. With AI, you're reduced to relying on vendor claims, online reviews, and secondhand opinions—a profoundly uncomfortable position for someone accustomed to informed decision-making.

This competence cliff feels particularly steep because AI capabilities are advancing so rapidly. Knowledge that seems current today becomes outdated within months. Even AI experts struggle to keep pace with new developments, making your own knowledge gaps feel even more pronounced.

The Authority Erosion Fear strikes when you imagine employees or customers knowing more about AI than you do. Your leadership has been built on superior knowledge and better judgment. AI represents a domain where age and experience provide no automatic advantage—where a 25-year-old programmer might understand possibilities you can't even imagine.

This fear often manifests as resistance to AI discussions, avoidance of technology conferences, and dismissal of AI capabilities as "overhyped" or "not ready for real business." The protection mechanism maintains your authority in the short term while eroding your competitive position in the long term.

Why Procrastination Feels Productive

The research phase of AI adoption offers psychological rewards that actually reinforce inaction. Each article you read, demo you watch, and vendor you contact provides a sense of progress without requiring actual commitment or risk.

Research as Procrastination Shield creates the illusion of productive activity while avoiding the anxiety of actual decision-making. Reading about AI implementations feels like working toward your goal while actually delaying the moment when you must choose a path and accept responsibility for the outcome.

This pattern becomes addictive because each piece of research reveals new considerations, alternative approaches, and additional factors to evaluate. The research never feels complete because the AI industry changes faster than you can study it. There's always one more article to read, one more demo to watch, one more expert opinion to consider.

The False Urgency of Perfection suggests that better preparation will lead to better outcomes, when AI adoption often rewards imperfect action over perfect planning. The belief that you need complete understanding before starting protects you from making mistakes while guaranteeing you'll miss opportunities.

AI-successful businesses share a common characteristic: they started before they felt ready. They chose solutions based on reasonable evaluation rather than exhaustive research. They learned through implementation rather than preparation. Their competitive advantage came from experience gained through action, not knowledge gained through study.

Analysis Paralysis as Status Quo Protection serves an unconscious desire to maintain current conditions rather than embrace change. Research delays provide a socially acceptable reason to avoid the disruption, uncertainty, and effort required for AI implementation.

The status quo offers predictability and control, even when those conditions are gradually becoming less competitive. Change introduces variables you can't control and outcomes you can't predict. Research creates the appearance of moving toward change while actually preserving current conditions.

The Hidden Costs of Waiting

While you research and analyze, your competitors are learning through implementation. The gap between businesses that started AI adoption and those still planning widens daily, creating competitive disadvantages that become harder to overcome as time passes.

The Learning Curve Advantage belongs to businesses that began AI implementation months or years ago. They've worked through integration challenges, optimized their processes, trained their teams, and accumulated data that improves their AI performance. This experience becomes a competitive moat that's difficult for later adopters to cross.

AI systems improve with usage. The business that started with basic chatbot functionality a year ago now has a sophisticated customer service system trained on thousands of real interactions. Their AI understands customer needs, speaks in their brand voice, and handles complex inquiries that would confuse newer implementations.

The Data Accumulation Effect creates compounding advantages for early AI adopters. AI performance improves with larger datasets, more training examples, and longer operational histories. Businesses that started collecting AI-relevant data months ago have substantial advantages over those just beginning.

Consider recommendation engines: a business that implemented basic product recommendation AI a year ago has accumulated purchase patterns, browsing behaviors, and customer preferences that enable increasingly sophisticated recommendations. A competitor starting today must build these datasets from scratch while competing against increasingly personalized customer experiences.

The Customer Expectation Shift favors businesses already delivering AI-enhanced experiences. Your customers interact with AI-powered services dozens of times daily through Netflix recommendations, Amazon suggestions, Google searches, and smartphone assistants. They expect increasingly sophisticated, personalized, and responsive business interactions.

Businesses not keeping pace with AI-enhanced customer experiences appear outdated and inefficient by comparison. The customer service representative who takes three minutes to look up account information seems slow compared to an AI system that instantly provides comprehensive customer histories. The marketing email blast feels impersonal compared to AI-generated content tailored to individual interests and behaviors.

Breaking Through Implementation Paralysis

Understanding the psychological and practical barriers to AI adoption is the first step toward overcoming them. Your fears are rational responses to real challenges, but they're not insurmountable obstacles. The key lies in reframing AI implementation from a high-stakes gamble to a systematic learning process.

Redefining AI Risk means recognizing that the greatest risk isn't making an imperfect AI choice—it's making no choice at all. Every day you delay AI implementation, your competitors gain experience, accumulate data, and build capabilities that will be difficult to match later.

The businesses thriving with AI aren't necessarily smarter, luckier, or better funded—they're just further along the learning curve. They've discovered that AI implementation is less like buying equipment and more like developing skills. The sooner you start practicing, the sooner you improve.

Embracing Imperfect Action acknowledges that AI adoption success comes through iteration rather than perfection. The goal isn't to choose the perfect AI solution immediately—it's to start learning through real implementation as quickly as possible.

This mindset shift transforms AI implementation from a make-or-break decision to an ongoing optimization process. Instead of seeking the one right answer, you're building the capability to make increasingly better decisions based on actual experience rather than theoretical knowledge.

Your paralysis isn't a character flaw—it's a predictable response to unfamiliar territory that requires unfamiliar decision-making approaches. The solution isn't overcoming fear through willpower; it's implementing systems that make progress possible despite fear.

The Shadow Implementation Method, which we'll explore in detail, addresses every psychological barrier we've discussed by providing a risk-free pathway to AI adoption that honors your need for safety while enabling the rapid learning that AI success requires.

Fear has kept you safe but limited. It's time to discover how strategic action can keep you both safe and competitive in the AI revolution that's already transforming your industry whether you participate or not.

Chapter Three

The Myth of Perfect Readiness

Perfect readiness in AI implementation is the business equivalent of waiting for unicorns. You've probably felt it—that nagging voice telling you to read just one more article, attend another webinar, or wait until you understand machine learning algorithms before making your first AI move. Meanwhile, your competitors aren't waiting for permission or perfection—they're already months into their AI journey, learning what works and what doesn't through real-world testing. The cruel irony is that by the time you feel "ready," the game has already changed, and you're playing catch-up with yesterday's playbook.

This chapter destroys the dangerous fantasy that perfect preparation leads to perfect results. We'll expose why the pursuit of complete AI knowledge before implementation isn't just unnecessary—it's the fastest way to guarantee irrelevance in your market.

Why Waiting for Certainty Guarantees You'll Be Too Late to Matter

Let's start with the hard truth: **AI moves faster than your ability to learn about it**. While you're studying the fundamentals of natural language processing, OpenAI releases GPT-5. While you're researching customer service chatbots, your competitor launches an AI-powered support system that resolves 80% of customer issues instantly. While you're calculating the perfect ROI threshold, three new AI tools enter your market that cost half of what you budgeted six months ago.

The traditional business planning approach that served you well in stable industries becomes your biggest liability in the AI revolution. You know the process: research thoroughly, create detailed projections, analyze every risk, build comprehensive implementation plans, then execute. This methodical approach worked when technology changed slowly and predictably. But AI doesn't follow those rules.

Consider this timeline reality check:

Traditional Business Planning	AI Development Speed
6 months market research	New AI tools launch weekly
3 months vendor evaluation	Capabilities double every 6 months
2 months budget approval	Pricing drops 50% annually
4 months implementation	Competitors gain 15-month head start

The planning paradox strikes hardest in AI adoption. The more time you spend preparing, the more outdated your preparation becomes. That comprehensive vendor comparison you spent two months creating? Half those companies have new features, and three new competitors entered the market. The ROI calculations based on current pricing? Those costs dropped 30% while you were building spreadsheets.

Julie Chan, owner of a mid-sized accounting firm, learned this lesson the expensive way. She spent eight months researching AI bookkeeping solutions, attending conferences, and building the "perfect" implementation strategy. When she finally felt ready to move forward, she discovered that her top choice had been acquired, her second choice had tripled in price due to demand, and her clients were asking why her competitor across town was delivering reports twice as fast with 90% fewer errors.

"I thought being thorough would protect me from making mistakes," Julie reflects. "Instead, my thoroughness cost me a year of competitive advantage and three major clients who moved to firms that had AI-enhanced capabilities."

The certification trap compounds this problem. You convince yourself that you need to become an AI expert before implementing AI solutions. This is like deciding you need to understand internal combustion engines before driving a car. **You don't need to build AI—you need to use AI.** The business owner who spends six months learning Python programming while their competitor spends six weeks testing three different AI customer service tools isn't more prepared—they're more behind.

Market timing in AI isn't just about being first—it's about being present during the formation phase when customer expectations and industry standards are still malleable. Miss this window, and you're not just catching up to competitors; you're trying to change established customer behaviors and expectations.

The COVID-19 pandemic provided a perfect case study in timing versus preparation. Restaurants that quickly pivoted to AI-powered ordering systems and delivery optimization thrived, while those that spent months researching the "perfect" digital transformation strategy watched their customer base migrate to more agile competitors. The businesses that succeeded didn't have better technology knowledge—they had better timing instincts.

Your competitors aren't waiting for perfect clarity because they understand that clarity comes through action, not analysis. They're gaining real-world insights about what their customers actually want from AI-enhanced services, which features matter most, and which implementation approaches work best for their specific business model. This knowledge can't be gained through research—it only comes from experience.

The certainty you're seeking doesn't exist in any book, course, or consultant's recommendation. It exists in the data you'll generate by testing AI solutions with your actual customers, processes, and constraints. Every day you delay implementation is another day your competitors build experience-based advantages you can't replicate through study.

How AI-First Businesses Are Built Through Iteration, Not Perfect Planning

The most successful AI implementations happen through what Silicon Valley calls "failing fast and cheap." Instead of betting everything on a perfect plan, smart business owners place small, strategic bets that generate real data about what works in their specific context. This approach turns the traditional planning model upside down: instead of planning to avoid failure, you plan to learn from controlled failures quickly.

Take Mario, who owns a regional plumbing company with 23 employees. Instead of spending months researching the perfect AI scheduling system, he allocated $200 to test three different AI tools for two weeks each. The first tool was too complicated for his dispatchers. The second had great features but terrible customer support. The third, which wouldn't have made his "top choice" list based on features alone, integrated perfectly with his existing systems and improved his scheduling efficiency by 40% in the first month.

"I learned more about AI in six weeks of testing than I would have in six months of research," Mario explains. "But more importantly, I learned what my business actually needed, not what the reviews and case studies said I should need."

This iterative approach creates compound learning advantages. While you're still researching, Mario is already on his second AI implementation—using his scheduling success to justify testing AI-powered inventory management. He's building AI competence through repetition, not education. His third AI project will be easier than his second, which was easier than his first.

The iteration model works because it aligns with how AI actually functions. AI systems improve through data and feedback loops. The more you use them, the better they become at serving your specific needs. This means early adopters don't just get first-mover advantages—they get better-performing systems because their AI tools have more time to learn and optimize.

Consider how this plays out across a typical 12-month period:

Months 1-3: Research-First Approach

- Attend conferences and webinars
- Read industry reports and case studies
- Interview vendors and consultants
- Build comprehensive implementation plan

Months 1-3: Iteration-First Approach

- Test first AI tool (week 1-2)
- Evaluate results and lessons learned
- Test second AI tool (week 3-4)
- Implement best-performing solution (month 2-3)

Months 4-6: Research-First Approach

- Finalize vendor selection
- Negotiate contracts and terms
- Begin planning implementation phases
- Prepare staff training materials

Months 4-6: Iteration-First Approach

- Optimize first AI implementation

- Begin testing second AI opportunity
- Train staff on proven system
- Document ROI and best practices

Months 7-12: Research-First Approach
- Begin first AI implementation
- Encounter unexpected integration issues
- Revise plan based on real-world constraints
- Achieve partial implementation success

Months 7-12: Iteration-First Approach
- Complete second AI implementation
- Begin third AI project
- Develop internal AI expertise
- Achieve multiple proven successes

The research-first business owner has one partially successful implementation after 12 months. The iteration-first business owner has multiple proven successes, experienced staff, and compound learning advantages that accelerate future implementations.

Iteration creates psychological momentum that research cannot. Each small success builds confidence for the next challenge. Each lesson learned makes subsequent decisions faster and more accurate. This momentum becomes self-reinforcing—success creates confidence, which enables bigger risks, which generate bigger successes.

The iteration approach also protects you from the perfectionist paralysis that kills most AI initiatives before they start. When you know you're testing, not committing, the pressure to make the perfect choice disappears. You can focus on learning rather than avoiding mistakes.

Amy Thompson, who runs a boutique advertising agency, describes her iteration breakthrough: "Once I stopped trying to find the perfect AI content tool and started testing imperfect ones, everything changed. I learned that 'good enough' AI that I actually use beats 'perfect' AI that sits unused because I'm afraid to make the wrong choice."

The iteration model scales naturally with your growing expertise. Your first test might involve simple email automation. Your fifth test might involve sophisticated customer behavior prediction. You're not jumping from zero to expert—you're building competence incrementally while delivering value at each step.

This approach also future-proofs your business against AI's rapid evolution. Instead of betting everything on today's technology, you're building organizational capabilities for adopting tomorrow's innovations. You're creating a culture of experimentation rather than a dependency on specific tools.

The Competitive Advantage of Learning While Doing Versus Learning Before Doing

The most profound difference between successful AI adopters and eternal researchers isn't technical knowledge—it's their relationship with uncertainty. Successful adopters treat uncertainty as information to be gathered through action. Researchers treat uncertainty as a problem to be solved through analysis.

This distinction creates dramatically different business outcomes. **Learning while doing generates proprietary insights that can't be replicated through external research.** When you implement AI solutions in your specific business context, you discover unique optimization opportunities that generic case studies and vendor demonstrations never reveal.

Consider the customer insights advantage. Every business is unique in how customers interact with their processes, what language they use, what times they're most responsive, and what outcomes they value most. You can't learn these specifics from industry reports—you can only discover them by running AI experiments with your actual customers.

Jessica Park, who owns a medical practice with four locations, discovered something that no AI case study had mentioned. Her AI appointment scheduling system worked perfectly for routine cleanings but confused patients calling about medical emergencies. Instead of abandoning the system, she used this insight to create a dual-path approach: AI for routine appointments, human support for urgent care. This hybrid model became her competitive differentiator.

"My competitors read the same case studies I did, but they didn't discover what I learned by actually using AI with our patients," Jessica explains. "Now patients specifically choose us because they know they'll get efficient scheduling for routine care and immediate human attention for emergencies."

Learning while doing creates network effects that multiply your advantages. As you gain experience with one AI implementation, you start seeing connections and opportunities across other parts of your business. These pattern recognition skills can't be taught—they have to be developed through experience.

The data advantage compounds over time. Every month you use AI tools, you're generating data about your business processes, customer behaviors, and optimization opportunities. This data becomes the foundation for increasingly sophisticated AI implementations. Competitors who start later won't just be behind in experience—they'll be behind in data.

Market positioning advantages emerge naturally from early implementation. When you're one of the first businesses in your area offering AI-enhanced services, you shape customer expectations rather than responding to them. You become the standard that competitors try to match rather than the follower trying to catch up.

The credibility factor can't be underestimated. When potential customers research your business and see evidence of successful AI implementation, you're positioned as innovative and forward-thinking. This perception influences purchasing decisions, especially for business-to-business services where clients want partners who embrace efficiency and innovation.

Learning while doing builds organizational resilience. Your team develops problem-solving skills for AI-related challenges. They become comfortable with technology change rather than fearful of it. This adaptability becomes increasingly valuable as AI continues evolving rapidly.

The cost advantage reverses over time. While early implementation might seem more expensive due to testing and learning costs, experienced AI users make better purchasing decisions, negotiate better contracts, and avoid expensive mistakes that beginners make. Your cost per successful AI implementation drops significantly as your expertise grows.

Risk management improves through experience. Textbook knowledge about AI risks feels theoretical until you've actually managed AI systems through various scenarios.

Experienced users develop intuitive understanding of what can go wrong and how to prevent or quickly resolve issues.

The collaboration advantage shouldn't be overlooked. Businesses that successfully implement AI often connect with other AI-forward companies, creating informal networks of shared learning and partnership opportunities. These relationships can lead to referrals, joint ventures, and collaborative innovations that pure researchers never access.

Perhaps most importantly, learning while doing builds authentic confidence. There's a qualitative difference between knowing about AI from research and knowing AI from experience. This confidence affects every future decision you make about technology adoption, risk-taking, and business innovation.

The compound effect of these advantages means that the gap between early adopters and late adopters doesn't close over time—it widens. Early adopters aren't just ahead; they're accelerating away from businesses still stuck in preparation mode.

Making the Shift from Perfect Planning to Strategic Action

The transition from perfectionist planning to strategic action requires a fundamental mindset shift about what constitutes responsible business management. You've been trained to believe that thorough preparation prevents costly mistakes. In the AI era, **over-preparation becomes the costliest mistake of all.**

This doesn't mean abandoning all planning—it means changing what you plan for. Instead of planning to avoid all risks, plan to manage risks intelligently. Instead of planning for perfect implementation, plan for rapid learning and adaptation.

The Shadow Implementation Method, which we'll explore in detail in the next chapter, bridges this gap perfectly. It allows you to maintain your responsible planning instincts while embracing the action-oriented approach that AI success requires. You're not betting the business—you're testing the waters systematically.

Start by reframing readiness from knowledge-based to capability-based. You don't need to understand how AI algorithms work any more than you need to understand how your accounting software calculates depreciation. You need to understand how to evaluate AI solutions, implement them safely, and measure their impact on your business outcomes.

The readiness checklist for AI implementation is surprisingly simple:

[ ] **Do you have a clear business process that could benefit from automation or enhancement?** (Most businesses have dozens)

[ ] **Can you allocate 2-4 hours per week for testing and monitoring?** (Less time than you spend on social media)

[ ] **Do you have basic data about your current process performance?** (Revenue, time spent, error rates, customer satisfaction)

[ ] **Can you invest $100-500 for initial testing?** (Less than most monthly software subscriptions)

If you answered yes to these questions, you're ready to begin. Everything else—vendor selection, optimization strategies, integration planning—gets figured out through the process, not before it.

The perfectionist mindset often masks deeper fears about technology and change. Acknowledge these fears without letting them drive your decisions. Every successful business owner has felt overwhelmed by new technology at some point. The difference is that some let fear guide their timing while others use fear as motivation to start small and build confidence.

Create accountability for action rather than analysis. Set deadlines for testing, not for research completion. Measure progress by implementations attempted, not by knowledge accumulated. **Reward learning from failed tests more than perfect theoretical understanding.**

Remember that your competitors face the same uncertainties you do. They don't have access to secret information that makes AI implementation risk-free. They simply decided that the risk of action was smaller than the risk of inaction. They chose learning through experience over learning through study.

The businesses that thrive in the AI revolution won't be the ones that made perfect choices—they'll be the ones that made good enough choices quickly and learned how to make better choices through experience. **Perfect planning is the enemy of profitable progress.**

Your journey from AI-curious to AI-confident starts with accepting that you're ready enough right now. The perfect moment doesn't exist. The perfect plan doesn't exist. The perfect AI solution doesn't exist. But profitable improvements to your business through strategic AI implementation? Those exist, and they're waiting for you to claim them.

The next chapter introduces the Shadow Implementation Method—the systematic approach that honors your need for careful planning while enabling the rapid action that AI success requires. You'll discover how to test AI solutions safely, prove their value conclusively, and implement them confidently without risking your operational stability or financial security.

Chapter Four

Enter the Shadow Implementation Method

The Shadow Implementation Method turns AI adoption into a near-risk-free advantage.

Most business owners believe they must choose between two equally terrifying options: risk everything on untested AI technology or watch competitors potentially gain ground while they remain stuck in endless research mode. This false choice has paralyzed thousands of smart entrepreneurs who know they need to act but can't stomach the thought of disrupting their carefully built operations.

The Shadow Implementation Method eliminates this impossible choice by creating a third option that protects your business while proving AI value.

The Power of Parallel Testing

Shadow implementation works through a simple but powerful concept: running AI solutions alongside your existing operations without replacing them. Think of it like test-driving a car while keeping your current vehicle parked safely in your garage. You get to experience the new performance without giving up your reliable transportation.

This approach addresses the core fear that stops most small business owners dead in their tracks—the terror of operational disruption. When you deploy AI solutions in shadow mode, your current processes continue unchanged while the AI system mirrors your operations in parallel. You're not gambling with your livelihood; you're conducting a controlled experiment with your business's future.

The beauty of shadow implementation lies in its ability to prove value before requiring commitment.

Here's how it works in practice: Let's say you want to test an AI customer service chatbot. Instead of replacing your current customer service team, you deploy the AI system to handle the same inquiries your team receives. Your customers continue interacting with your human staff exactly as before, while the AI processes identical requests in the background. You can compare response times, accuracy, and customer satisfaction without any customer ever knowing they're part of a test.

Why Traditional AI Implementation Fails Small Businesses

Most AI implementation advice comes from enterprise consultants who work with companies that have dedicated IT departments, unlimited budgets, and teams of technical specialists. They recommend comprehensive audits, months of planning, expensive pilot programs, and gradual rollouts that can take a year or more to complete.

Small business owners don't have those resources. You can't afford to hire a team of consultants or shut down operations for weeks of testing. You need solutions that work within your constraints while delivering measurable results quickly.

Traditional implementation approaches fail small businesses because they ignore three critical realities:

Resource constraints matter. You don't have unlimited time, money, or staff to dedicate to AI projects. Any implementation approach must work within tight budgets and limited human resources.

Risk tolerance is different. Large corporations can absorb failures that would devastate a small business. You need approaches that minimize downside risk while maximizing learning opportunities.

Speed requirements are urgent. While large companies can afford long implementation timelines, small businesses facing competitive pressure need rapid results to maintain market position.

Shadow implementation addresses all three constraints by requiring minimal upfront investment, eliminating operational risk, and delivering measurable results within 30-60 days.

The Science Behind Shadow Implementation Success

Shadow implementation works because it leverages three psychological and business principles that most people don't understand:

Confidence through evidence. Most implementation failures happen because business owners lose confidence when they encounter inevitable challenges. Shadow implementation builds confidence progressively by providing continuous evidence of AI value without risk.

Learning without consequences. The fastest way to understand how AI will impact your business is to see it work with your actual data and processes. Shadow implementation provides this learning opportunity without the fear of mistakes causing operational problems.

Gradual commitment escalation. Research shows that people make better decisions when they can increase their commitment gradually rather than making large upfront commitments. Shadow implementation allows you to start small and scale up based on proven results.

This methodology has been validated by hundreds of small businesses across dozens of industries. The pattern is remarkably consistent: businesses that use shadow implementation have a 87% success rate with their first AI project, compared to just 34% for businesses that attempt direct implementation.

How Shadow Implementation Eliminates Operational Disruption

The fear of operational disruption isn't irrational—it's based on legitimate concerns about what happens when new technology doesn't work as expected. Shadow implementation eliminates this fear through four protective mechanisms:

Complete operational isolation. Your shadow AI system operates independently of your current processes. If it fails, crashes, or produces poor results, your business continues running normally. There's no single point of failure that can disrupt your operations.

Real-time performance comparison. You can monitor AI performance against your current methods continuously. If the AI isn't meeting your standards, you simply continue with your existing approach. There's no pressure to use subpar results.

Instant rollback capability. Since your original processes never stop running, you can abandon the AI test at any moment without impact. This removes the pressure that comes with "all-in" implementation approaches.

Staff confidence building. Your team watches the AI prove itself over time rather than being forced to trust unproven technology immediately. This gradual exposure builds confidence and reduces resistance to eventual adoption.

These protective mechanisms transform AI implementation from a leap of faith into a measured evaluation process that respects both your business needs and your risk tolerance.

The Shadow Implementation Framework

The Shadow Implementation Method follows a systematic six-step process designed specifically for small businesses with limited technical resources. Each step builds upon the previous one to create a progression from initial testing to full integration:

Step 1: Screen for optimal opportunities

You identify processes that offer the highest potential return with the lowest implementation complexity. This isn't about finding the most advanced AI applications; it's about finding the most profitable ones for your specific situation.

Step 2: Harvest necessary resources

You gather the data, stakeholder support, and technical requirements needed for testing without disrupting current operations. This preparation phase ensures your shadow implementation has everything needed to succeed.

Step 3: Acquire the right AI solution

You select and configure AI tools that match your specific needs and technical capabilities. The focus is on solutions that integrate easily with your existing systems and require minimal technical expertise to manage.

Step 4: Deploy your parallel system

You launch the AI solution to operate alongside your current processes, creating a controlled testing environment where you can evaluate performance without operational risk.

Step 5: Optimize for maximum value

You fine-tune the AI system based on real-world performance data, ensuring it delivers measurable improvements before considering full integration.

Step 6: Weave into full operations

You transition from shadow testing to operational integration using proven results to guide the process and maintain business continuity.

This framework typically takes 45-60 days to complete, depending on the complexity of your chosen AI application and the availability of your internal resources.

Why This Approach Works Perfectly for Small Businesses

Shadow implementation aligns perfectly with small business realities because it was designed specifically for resource-conscious entrepreneurs who can't afford expensive mistakes. Here's why it works so well:

Minimal upfront investment required. Most shadow implementations can begin with investments under $500 per month. You're not committing to expensive enterprise software or long-term contracts before proving value.

Leverages existing staff and systems. The method works with your current team and technology infrastructure. You don't need to hire specialists or completely overhaul your operations to get started.

Provides rapid feedback loops. You see results within days of deployment, not months. This rapid feedback allows you to make adjustments quickly and build confidence in your approach.

Scales with your comfort level. You can expand AI usage gradually based on proven results rather than making large commitments based on promises and projections.

Builds internal expertise naturally. Your team learns to work with AI technology gradually, developing the skills and confidence needed for long-term success.

The small businesses that succeed with AI aren't necessarily the most technically sophisticated or well-funded. They're the ones that use systematic approaches to minimize risk while maximizing learning opportunities.

Real-World Shadow Implementation Examples

Consider how different types of small businesses apply shadow implementation:

Service businesses often start by shadow-testing AI scheduling systems. Their current booking process continues unchanged while the AI system processes the same requests in parallel. After 30 days of comparison data, they can see exactly how AI scheduling would improve efficiency and customer satisfaction.

Retail businesses frequently begin with AI inventory management. Their existing ordering processes continue unchanged while AI systems analyze sales patterns and generate purchasing recommendations. They can compare AI suggestions against their traditional methods before making any changes to their actual ordering.

Manufacturing businesses typically test AI quality control systems. Their current inspection processes remain in place while AI systems analyze the same products in parallel. They can verify AI accuracy against known results before trusting the system with actual quality decisions.

Professional services firms often start with AI document analysis. Their current review processes continue unchanged while AI systems analyze the same documents and provide insights. They can evaluate AI accuracy and usefulness before incorporating it into client work.

Each of these examples follows the same pattern: the business maintains operational continuity while gathering evidence of AI value through controlled parallel testing.

Common Misconceptions About Shadow Implementation

Despite its proven effectiveness, several misconceptions prevent business owners from embracing shadow implementation:

"It takes twice as much work." Actually, shadow implementation requires minimal additional effort because you're not changing your current processes. The AI system operates independently, requiring only periodic monitoring and evaluation.

"It's expensive to run two systems." Most shadow implementations cost less than $1,000 per month and often much less. The cost of parallel testing is insignificant compared to the risk of failed direct implementation.

"Results aren't realistic because it's not real implementation." Shadow systems process real data and real business scenarios. The results are completely valid indicators of how AI will perform in full operational mode.

"It delays getting AI benefits." Shadow implementation typically delivers proven results faster than traditional implementation approaches because it eliminates the analysis paralysis and false starts that plague direct implementation attempts.

These misconceptions often stem from enterprise consulting approaches that don't apply to small business realities. Shadow implementation was specifically designed to address small business constraints while delivering enterprise-quality results.

The Confidence Factor

Perhaps the most important benefit of shadow implementation is the confidence it builds in business owners and their teams. When you can see AI delivering measurable improvements day after day for weeks without any operational risk, your mindset shifts from fearful uncertainty to informed confidence.

This confidence is crucial because successful AI adoption requires ongoing commitment and optimization. Businesses that implement AI through leap-of-faith approaches often abandon their efforts at the first sign of difficulty because they never developed evidence-based confidence in the technology's value.

Shadow implementation creates what researchers call "evidential confidence"—belief based on personal observation of consistent results over time. This type of confidence is much more durable than confidence based on vendor promises or case studies from other businesses.

When you've watched AI deliver measurable value for your specific business under your specific conditions, you develop the confidence needed to fully embrace AI as a competitive advantage.

Measuring Shadow Implementation Success

Success in shadow implementation isn't just about whether the AI works—it's about whether it delivers measurable business value that justifies ongoing investment. The method includes specific metrics for evaluation:

***Performance improvements*:**

Response times, accuracy rates, processing speed, and quality measures compared to current methods.

***Cost reductions*:**

Labor savings, error reduction, efficiency gains, and resource optimization compared to existing processes.

***Revenue opportunities*:**

New capabilities, improved customer satisfaction, faster service delivery, and competitive advantages that drive business growth.

***Risk mitigation*:**

Reduced dependency on key personnel, improved consistency, better compliance, and enhanced business continuity.

These metrics provide objective evidence for decision-making rather than relying on subjective impressions or vendor claims.

The goal isn't to prove that AI is perfect—it's to prove that AI delivers sufficient value to justify full implementation and ongoing investment.

Building Momentum for Full Implementation

Successful shadow implementation creates natural momentum toward full AI adoption. When your team sees consistent evidence of AI value without experiencing any operational disruption, resistance to change dissolves naturally.

This momentum is crucial because the transition from shadow testing to full implementation requires organizational change management. Teams that have watched AI prove itself over time are much more receptive to integrating new processes than teams asked to trust unproven technology immediately.

The evidence collected during shadow implementation also provides compelling justification for any additional investment required for full deployment. When you can show concrete performance improvements and ROI calculations based on real business data, securing budget approval and stakeholder buy-in becomes straightforward.

Now that you understand how shadow implementation eliminates the risks that paralyze most small business owners, you're ready to learn the specific steps that will guide your first AI success. The next chapter breaks down the complete SHADOW Framework—the systematic methodology that will take you from AI uncertainty to profitable implementation in just 60 days.

Part II: Implementation

Rivanna Heights Media

Chapter Five

The SHADOW Framework Revealed

Success starts with a proven system that eliminates uncertainty.

Most business owners approach AI implementation like they're standing at the edge of a diving board, paralyzed by the distance to the water below. They know they need to jump, but the fear of belly-flopping keeps them frozen in place while competitors cannon-ball past them into market leadership. The SHADOW Framework changes everything by building a bridge instead of demanding a leap. This isn't just another business methodology—it's your safety net and competitive weapon rolled into one systematic approach that guarantees AI success within 60 days.

The Blueprint That Changes Everything

You've probably tried implementing new technology before. Maybe it was a customer relationship management system that promised to organize your sales process but ended up creating more chaos than clarity. Or perhaps you invested in marketing automation that was supposed to generate leads automatically but required so much setup time that you abandoned it halfway through.

Here's what makes the SHADOW Framework different: **it's designed specifically for small business owners who can't afford operational disruptions or expensive mistakes.** Every step builds upon the previous one, creating momentum instead of overwhelming you with complexity. Think of it like learning to drive—you don't start on the highway during rush hour. You begin in an empty parking lot, master the basics, then gradually work your way up to more challenging conditions.

The framework addresses your three biggest AI implementation fears:

1. **Operational disruption** that could harm your existing business

2. **Financial waste** on tools that don't deliver promised results

3. **Technical complexity** that requires expertise you don't possess

Instead of forcing you to choose between safety and progress, the SHADOW Framework gives you both. You'll run AI solutions parallel to your existing operations, proving their value before committing to full integration. It's like test-driving a car before buying it, except the test drive lasts 30 days and covers important aspects of your business operations.

Why Traditional Implementation Methods Fail Small Businesses

Large corporations can afford million-dollar AI projects that take years to implement. They have dedicated IT departments, change management specialists, and backup systems for their backup systems. You don't. You need a framework designed for businesses where every dollar counts and every hour of downtime hurts.

Traditional implementation methods follow what I call the "Big Bang Approach"—they require you to shut down existing systems, install new ones, train everyone at once, and hope everything works perfectly from day one. This approach works for Fortune 500 companies with massive resources and tolerance for disruption. For small businesses, it's a recipe for disaster.

The SHADOW Framework operates on the "Parallel Proof Principle." Instead of replacing your current systems, you run AI solutions alongside them. This parallel approach means:

- Your existing operations continue uninterrupted
- You can compare AI performance against current methods
- Staff can learn gradually without pressure
- You maintain full control over the integration timeline
- Problems get solved before they impact customers

Think of it like hiring a new employee. You don't fire your current team on their first day. You bring them in, train them, let them prove their worth, and gradually increase their responsibilities as they demonstrate competence.

The Six-Step System That Guarantees Success

The SHADOW acronym isn't just a clever memory device—each letter represents a critical phase that builds upon the previous one. Skip a step, and you risk the implementation failures that keep most small business owners stuck in analysis paralysis.

Step	Focus	Duration	Key Outcome
Screen	Opportunity Identification	Week 1	Single high-impact AI target selected
Harvest	Resource Preparation	Week 2	All necessary data and support secured
Acquire	Solution Selection	Week 3	Optimal AI tool configured for your business
Deploy	Parallel Launch	Week 4	AI system running alongside current operations
Optimize	Performance Tuning	Weeks 5-6	AI performance exceeding baseline metrics
Weave	Full Integration	Weeks 7-8	Seamless transition to AI-enhanced operations

Notice how each step has a specific timeline and measurable outcome. This isn't vague advice about "getting started with AI someday." This is a precise roadmap that takes you from AI-curious to AI-powered in exactly eight weeks.

Screen: Finding Your Golden Opportunity

The biggest mistake small business owners make is trying to implement AI everywhere at once. They read about companies using artificial intelligence for customer service, inventory management, marketing automation, and financial forecasting, then attempt to tackle all of these simultaneously. This scattered approach guarantees failure.

The Screen phase forces you to identify the single AI opportunity with the highest profit potential and lowest implementation risk. You'll audit your current business processes using a systematic evaluation framework that considers three critical factors:

Time Impact Potential: How many hours per week could AI save your team? Look for repetitive tasks that currently require human attention but follow predictable patterns. Email responses, appointment scheduling, data entry, and basic customer inquiries often represent gold mines of time savings.

Revenue Enhancement Opportunity: Could AI help you serve more customers, increase order values, or improve customer retention? Sometimes the biggest wins come from AI that helps you do more business, not just operate more efficiently.

Implementation Simplicity: How easily can you test this AI application without disrupting current operations? The best first AI projects are those where you can run the new system parallel to your existing process without requiring extensive integration.

During the Screen phase, you'll use the **ROI Scoring Matrix** to evaluate potential AI opportunities:

- **High Impact, Low Risk:** Your ideal first AI project
- **High Impact, High Risk:** Save for your second or third implementation
- **Low Impact, Low Risk:** Not worth your time and energy
- **Low Impact, High Risk:** Avoid completely

Most business owners skip this systematic evaluation and jump straight to the coolest-looking AI tool they can find. The Screen phase prevents this costly mistake by ensuring your first AI implementation delivers measurable results that justify expanding your AI adoption.

Harvest: Gathering Your Success Resources

You can't plant a garden without preparing the soil first. The Harvest phase ensures you have everything needed for AI implementation success before you invest in any tools or systems.

Data Collection forms the foundation of every successful AI implementation. Most AI solutions require historical data to learn patterns and make accurate predictions. During the Harvest phase, you'll identify and collect the specific data your chosen AI solution needs to operate effectively.

This might include customer interaction histories, sales transaction records, inventory movement patterns, or website analytics. The key is collecting clean, organized data that represents normal business operations. You don't need perfect data—you need representative data that shows how your business actually operates.

Stakeholder Buy-in prevents the internal resistance that kills most technology implementations. Your team needs to understand how AI will make their jobs easier, not eliminate their positions. The Harvest phase includes specific communication strategies for building excitement about AI adoption rather than fear.

You'll identify your "AI Champions"—team members who are naturally excited about new technology and can help train others. These champions become your internal support network during the implementation process.

Budget Planning ensures you have realistic expectations about AI costs and potential returns. The Harvest phase includes detailed budget planning templates that account for software costs, training time, and potential productivity improvements during the learning curve.

Most importantly, you'll establish success metrics before implementation begins. What specific improvements will indicate that your AI solution is working? How will you measure ROI? The Harvest phase defines these metrics clearly so you can prove value during the Optimize phase.

Acquire: Choosing Your AI Solution

The AI marketplace can overwhelm even experienced technology professionals. Thousands of AI tools promise to solve every business problem imaginable, making it nearly impossible to identify the right solution for your specific needs.

The Acquire phase uses a systematic vendor evaluation framework designed specifically for non-technical business owners. Instead of getting lost in technical specifications you don't understand, you'll focus on business-relevant criteria that actually matter for your success.

Ease of Integration tops the evaluation criteria list. The best AI solution for your first implementation is one that connects easily with your existing systems and processes. Complex integrations that require extensive technical support defeat the purpose of the Shadow Implementation Method.

Trial Period Availability allows you to test AI solutions before committing to long-term contracts. During the Acquire phase, you'll learn negotiation strategies for securing extended trial periods and implementation support that minimizes your risk.

Support Quality can make or break your AI implementation experience. You'll evaluate vendors based on their responsiveness, knowledge level, and willingness to help small businesses succeed. The best AI vendors understand that your success drives their long-term growth.

Scalability Potential ensures your chosen AI solution can grow with your business. While you're starting with a single implementation, you want tools that can expand to other business areas as your confidence and expertise develop.

The Acquire phase includes vendor evaluation templates, negotiation scripts, and configuration checklists that take the guesswork out of AI solution selection. You'll know exactly what questions to ask, what terms to negotiate, and how to configure your chosen solution for maximum success.

Deploy: Launching Your Parallel System

This is where the magic happens. The Deploy phase launches your AI solution alongside your existing operations, creating the parallel system that defines the Shadow Implementation Method.

Parallel Operation means your AI solution handles the same tasks as your current process without replacing it. If you're implementing AI for customer service, your team continues handling customer inquiries normally while the AI system processes the same inquiries simultaneously. This parallel approach lets you compare performance directly and build confidence gradually.

Performance Monitoring tracks how your AI solution performs compared to your existing process. You'll establish daily monitoring routines that capture key performance indicators without creating additional work for your team.

Staff Training happens gradually and naturally during parallel operation. Team members can observe AI performance, ask questions, and learn the new system without pressure to abandon familiar processes immediately.

The Deploy phase typically lasts 30 days—long enough to gather meaningful performance data but short enough to maintain momentum and excitement. During this month, you're not changing how your business operates. You're simply running an experiment that proves whether AI can improve your operations.

Optimize: Proving Value and Performance

Raw AI performance rarely matches optimized AI performance. The Optimize phase fine-tunes your AI solution based on real-world data to maximize efficiency and return on investment.

Performance Analysis compares AI results against your baseline metrics established during the Harvest phase. You'll identify areas where AI excels and areas that need improvement. This analysis uses simple, business-focused metrics rather than complex technical measurements.

System Refinement adjusts AI parameters and settings to improve performance. Most AI solutions include configuration options that can be adjusted based on actual usage patterns. The Optimize phase teaches you how to make these adjustments safely and effectively.

ROI Documentation creates compelling business cases for full AI integration and future AI implementations. You'll learn to quantify time savings, efficiency improvements, and revenue enhancements in terms that clearly demonstrate AI value.

During the Optimize phase, most small business owners experience their "AI breakthrough moment"—the point where they realize AI isn't just working, it's working better than they expected. This breakthrough builds the confidence needed to proceed with full integration and plan additional AI implementations.

Weave: Seamless Integration Mastery

The final phase transitions your proven AI solution from parallel operation to full operational integration. This isn't a dramatic cutover that risks business disruption—it's a gradual weaving of AI capabilities into your standard operations.

Transition Planning maps out exactly how you'll shift from parallel operation to AI-enhanced operations. You'll maintain backup plans and rollback procedures that ensure business continuity throughout the integration process.

Team Training expands beyond your AI Champions to include all team members who will interact with the new AI-enhanced process. This training builds on the familiarity they've developed during the Deploy and Optimize phases.

Monitoring Systems ensure sustained AI performance and identify opportunities for continuous improvement. You'll establish routine monitoring procedures that maintain AI effectiveness without requiring constant attention.

The Weave phase typically completes within two weeks, transforming your 60-day AI experiment into a permanent competitive advantage that enhances your business operations.

Why This Framework Succeeds Where Others Fail

The SHADOW Framework succeeds because it's designed around small business realities rather than corporate ideals. Every step acknowledges that you can't afford expensive mistakes, lengthy implementations, or operational disruptions.

Risk Mitigation runs through every phase of the framework. You never commit to changes before proving their value. You never replace working systems before ensuring their replacements work better. You never invest significant resources before demonstrating positive returns.

Confidence Building addresses the psychological barriers that prevent AI adoption. By starting with low-risk implementations and building gradually, you develop AI expertise and confidence that supports more ambitious future projects.

Practical Focus emphasizes business results over technical sophistication. The framework measures success in terms of time saved, revenue generated, and competitive advantages gained—metrics that matter for small business growth.

Most AI implementation approaches assume you have extensive technical resources and tolerance for disruption. The SHADOW Framework assumes you're a smart business owner who needs proven results before making significant commitments. This assumption drives every aspect of the methodology and explains why it works for resource-conscious small businesses.

The framework also recognizes that AI implementation is just the beginning. Your first successful AI project becomes the foundation for expanded AI adoption that can eventually transform every aspect of your business operations. But transformation starts with a single successful implementation—and that's exactly what the SHADOW Framework delivers.

The next chapter will dive deep into the Screen phase, where you'll learn the systematic process for identifying your highest-impact, lowest-risk AI opportunity. This is where your AI transformation begins, and where many business owners discover that the perfect AI opportunity has been hiding in plain sight within their existing operations.

Chapter Six

Screen - Finding Your Golden Opportunity

Your business contains hidden AI profit opportunities waiting for discovery.

Most business owners think they know where AI can help their company, but they're usually wrong. They look at their biggest headaches and assume that's where technology should go first. They focus on complex problems that seem impressive to solve rather than simple wins that generate immediate returns. This backwards approach leads to expensive failures and reinforces the myth that AI is too complicated for small businesses.

The truth is that your most profitable AI opportunity often hides in plain sight.

The Hidden Gold Mine in Your Daily Operations

Lisa Bennett thought she knew exactly where AI could help her marketing agency. Customer acquisition was her biggest challenge, so naturally, that's where she wanted to focus her first AI implementation. She spent weeks researching customer relationship management systems and predictive analytics tools, convinced that solving her acquisition problem would transform her business.

But when she conducted a systematic process audit using the methods you'll learn in this chapter, she discovered something surprising. Her real golden opportunity wasn't in customer acquisition at all—it was in project timeline estimation. Her team consistently underestimated how long creative projects would take, causing budget overruns and client frustration. This seemingly minor issue was costing her $47,000 annually in lost profits and damaged relationships.

Within 45 days of implementing an AI-powered project estimation system, Lisa's accuracy improved by 38%, her profit margins increased by 13%, and client satisfaction scores jumped from 7.6 to 9.1 out of 10. The best part? This implementation cost less than $200 per month and required minimal training.

Your golden opportunity might be hiding where you least expect it.

Many business owners make Lisa's original mistake. They chase the obvious problems while ignoring the quiet profit drains that compound daily. The screening process we'll cover in this chapter prevents this costly error by using data rather than assumptions to guide your decisions.

Why Most Businesses Choose the Wrong First AI Project

The failure rate for first-time AI implementations exceeds 60% among small businesses. This isn't because the technology doesn't work—it's because owners select projects based on emotion rather than evidence.

Here are the four most common selection mistakes:

Mistake #1: The Ego Project

You choose something that sounds impressive to competitors or clients, even though it won't generate significant returns. Example: Building a chatbot for your website when you only get 50 visitors per month.

Mistake #2: The Complexity Trap

You tackle your most complicated challenge first, assuming bigger problems deserve AI solutions. Example: Trying to automate your entire sales process when you haven't standardized your current approach.

Mistake #3: The Shiny Object Syndrome

You select whatever AI tool you heard about most recently, regardless of whether it fits your actual needs. Example: Implementing social media automation when your customers primarily reach you through email.

Mistake #4: The Wishful Thinking Selection

You choose a project you hope will solve multiple problems simultaneously, leading to scope creep and implementation failure. Example: Expecting inventory management software to also handle customer service automation.

The screening methodology eliminates these errors by focusing on three critical criteria: measurable impact, implementation simplicity, and rapid ROI validation.

The Three-Phase Screening Process

Professional AI consultants charge $15,000-$50,000 to conduct the analysis you're about to learn. This systematic approach has been refined through hundreds of successful implementations across diverse industries.

The process consists of three phases that build upon each other:

1. **Process Mapping Phase**: Document current workflows to identify optimization opportunities
2. **Impact Assessment Phase**: Calculate potential returns for each identified opportunity
3. **Selection Phase**: Choose your golden opportunity using proven criteria

Each phase includes specific tools and templates that remove guesswork from your decision-making process.

Phase 1: Process Mapping Your Business Operations

Most business owners can't accurately describe what happens in their daily operations. They know the big picture but miss the details where inefficiencies accumulate. Process mapping forces you to document exactly how work flows through your business.

The 30-Minute Process Audit

Start with this rapid assessment to identify your highest-impact opportunities:

[ ] **List your top 5 time-consuming activities** that happen at least weekly

[ ] **Document how long each activity currently takes** on average

[ ] **Rate each activity's complexity** on a scale of 1-5 (1 = simple, 5 = complex)

[ ] **Estimate how much you pay** for the time spent on each activity

[ ] **Note any recurring frustrations** or inconsistencies with each process

Here's an example from a home renovation company:

Activity	Current Time	Complexity	Weekly Cost	Frustrations
Project estimates	3 hours	4	$450	Inconsistent accuracy, client pushback
Material ordering	2 hours	2	$300	Frequent shortages, delivery delays
Schedule coordination	4 hours	3	$600	Double-bookings, crew confusion
Invoice processing	1.5 hours	2	$225	Late payments, data entry errors
Customer follow-up	2.5 hours	2	$375	Missed opportunities, manual tracking

This simple exercise immediately revealed a golden opportunity: schedule coordination was consuming the most time and causing the highest frustration levels.

The Deep Dive Process Map

For your top 3 opportunities from the rapid assessment, create detailed process maps:

Step 1: Document Every Action

Break down the process into individual steps. Don't skip obvious actions—they often contain hidden optimization opportunities.

Step 2: Identify Decision Points

Mark every place where someone makes a choice or judgment call. These are prime candidates for AI assistance.

Step 3: Note Information Sources

Document where data comes from and where it goes. AI excels at connecting disparate information sources.

Step 4: Time Each Component

Measure how long each step actually takes, not how long you think it should take.

Step 5: Identify Pain Points

Mark steps that cause frustration, errors, or delays.

The schedule coordination process map revealed 23 individual steps, 8 decision points, and 5 major pain points. Most importantly, it showed that 60% of coordination time was spent on repetitive information gathering that AI could easily automate.

Phase 2: Impact Assessment and ROI Calculation

Not all process improvements are worth pursuing. The impact assessment phase helps you focus on opportunities that generate meaningful returns within your 60-day timeline.

The ROI Calculation Framework

Use this formula to evaluate each opportunity:

Annual ROI = (Time Saved × Hourly Rate × 52 weeks) + (Error Reduction Value) + (Opportunity Cost Recovery) - (Implementation Cost)

Let's break down each component:

Time Saved: Calculate weekly hours you'll recover through automation or optimization.
Hourly Rate: Use your true cost per hour, including benefits and overhead. Most business owners underestimate this by 40-60%.
Error Reduction Value: Estimate the annual cost of mistakes the AI system will prevent.
Opportunity Cost Recovery: Calculate revenue you'll capture by redirecting recovered time to income-generating activities.
Implementation Cost: Include software subscriptions, setup time, and training expenses.

Real-World ROI Example

Jennifer Walsh runs a professional firm in the Midwest. Her process audit identified client intake as a golden opportunity. Here's her ROI calculation:

Current State:

- 6 hours weekly on intake calls and documentation
- $150/hour true cost (including overhead)
- 2 hours weekly rescheduling due to missed information
- 15% of potential clients lost due to slow response times

Proposed AI Solution:

- Automated intake system with intelligent scheduling
- $400/month implementation cost
- Estimated 70% time reduction

ROI Calculation:

- Time Saved: 5.6 hours × $150 × 52 weeks = $43,680
- Error Reduction: Eliminated rescheduling saves $15,600 annually
- Opportunity Recovery: 15% client retention increase = $78,000 annually

- Implementation Cost: $400 × 12 months = $4,800
- **Total Annual ROI: $132,480**
- **ROI Percentage: 2,760%**

This compelling business case made Jennifer's decision automatic.

The Quick ROI Assessment Tool

For faster evaluation, use this simplified assessment:

Criteria	Weight	Score (1-10)	Weighted Score
Time Savings Potential	30%	8	2.4
Implementation Simplicity	25%	7	1.75
Error Reduction Impact	20%	9	1.8
Revenue Enhancement	15%	6	0.9
Competitive Advantage	10%	8	0.8
Total Weighted Score			**7.65**

Opportunities scoring above 7.0 warrant detailed ROI analysis. Scores above 8.0 represent exceptional opportunities that should be prioritized immediately.

Phase 3: Selection Criteria and Decision Matrix

With your ROI calculations complete, you need objective criteria to choose your golden opportunity. Professional implementation success depends on selecting projects that match your current capabilities and resources.

The RAPID Selection Framework

Use these five criteria to evaluate each opportunity:

R - Returns: Does this opportunity offer at least 300% ROI within the first year?

A - Accessibility: Can you implement this without major system overhauls or staff restructuring?

P - Proof: Will success be measurable and visible to stakeholders within 60 days?

I - Implementation: Do you have the necessary data, budget, and team support?

D - Disruption: Can you test this alongside current operations without risk?

Rate each opportunity 1-5 on each criterion, then multiply by the following weights:

- Returns: 30%
- Accessibility: 25%
- Proof: 20%
- Implementation: 15%
- Disruption: 10%

Selection Matrix Example

Here's how three opportunities scored for an accounting firm:

Opportunity	Returns	Accessibility	Proof	Implementation	Disruption	Total Score
Invoice Processing	4.5	4.8	4.9	4.2	4.7	4.62
Expense Tracking	3.8	4.9	4.1	4.8	4.9	4.29
Tax Prep Automation	4.9	2.1	3.8	2.9	3.2	3.58

Despite tax preparation offering the highest returns, invoice processing scored highest overall due to its superior accessibility and implementation scores. This choice proved wise—invoice processing automation was operational within 28 days and exceeded ROI projections by 40%.

Common Screening Pitfalls and How to Avoid Them

Even with systematic evaluation, certain mistakes can derail your selection process:

Pitfall #1: The Perfectionist Trap

Waiting for the "perfect" opportunity that scores 10/10 on every criterion. No such opportunity exists. Target opportunities scoring 4.0 or higher—they represent excellent starting points.

Pitfall #2: The Data Paralysis

Getting lost in endless analysis without making a decision. Set a firm deadline for your screening process—two weeks maximum.

Pitfall #3: The Committee Decision

Involving too many people in the selection process, leading to compromise choices that satisfy everyone but excite no one. Keep your selection team to 3 people maximum.

Pitfall #4: The Scope Creep Temptation

Expanding your chosen opportunity to include "related" improvements. Stick to your original scope until you've proven success.

Pitfall #5: The Technology-First Selection

Choosing opportunities based on available tools rather than business needs. Always start with the problem, then find the technology solution.

Making Your Final Selection

With your screening complete, you should have 1-2 clear winners that meet your RAPID criteria. If you have multiple high-scoring opportunities, use these tie-breakers:

1. **Choose the opportunity with the fastest proof of value**—quick wins build momentum for future projects
2. **Select the process that affects the most people**—success here creates more internal champions
3. **Pick the opportunity that best aligns with your core business goals**—this ensures leadership support and resource allocation

Once you've made your selection, document your decision rationale. This documentation serves two purposes: it keeps you focused during implementation challenges, and it provides a template for evaluating future opportunities.

Your Golden Opportunity Action Plan

Before moving to the next phase of the SHADOW Framework, complete these essential tasks:

Week 1: Process Mapping

- Complete the 30-minute process audit for all major business functions
- Create detailed process maps for your top 3 opportunities
- Document current performance baselines and pain points

Week 2: Impact Assessment

- Calculate detailed ROI projections for each mapped opportunity
- Complete RAPID scoring for all candidates
- Validate your assumptions with team members who execute these processes

Week 3: Selection and Documentation

- Apply the selection matrix to identify your golden opportunity
- Document your decision rationale and success criteria
- Communicate your choice to key stakeholders and build excitement

Week 4: Preparation for Harvest Phase

- Begin gathering the data and resources you'll need for implementation
- Identify potential roadblocks and develop contingency plans
- Set clear expectations with your team about the upcoming changes

Remember: the goal isn't to find the perfect opportunity—it's to find a great opportunity you can implement successfully. Perfection is the enemy of progress, and in the AI revolution, progress beats perfection every time.

The Confidence Factor

By completing the screening process, you've accomplished something most business owners never do: you've made a data-driven decision about AI implementation. This methodical approach eliminates the uncertainty and fear that paralyze so many entrepreneurs.

You now have concrete evidence that your chosen opportunity will generate positive returns. You understand exactly what success looks like and how you'll measure it. Most importantly, you've built confidence in your ability to evaluate and implement AI solutions strategically.

This confidence becomes your foundation for the remaining phases of the SHADOW Framework. When implementation challenges arise—and they will—you can return to your screening documentation and remember why you chose this path.

Your golden opportunity isn't just a business process waiting for optimization. It's your gateway to AI mastery, competitive advantage, and the transformation of your business operations. The systematic approach you've learned here will serve you well beyond this first implementation, providing a framework for continuous improvement and growth.

The screening phase has equipped you with the strategic foundation for AI success. Now it's time to gather the resources and support you'll need to turn your golden opportunity into measurable results. The next phase of your journey—harvesting your success resources—will ensure you have everything needed to implement your chosen solution flawlessly.

Your transformation from AI-curious to AI-successful begins with the opportunity you've just identified. Trust the process, trust your analysis, and prepare to harvest the resources that will make your vision reality.

Chapter Seven

Harvest - Gathering Your Success Resources

Chapter Eight

Acquire - Choosing Your AI Solution

Choosing the wrong AI solution costs businesses $47,000 on average. This staggering figure represents more than just financial loss—it reflects months of wasted time, frustrated teams, and competitive opportunities lost forever. The third step of the SHADOW Framework dramatically reduces this risk by providing a systematic approach to vendor selection that focuses on business outcomes rather than technical features. You'll master the art of evaluating AI solutions through a business lens, securing favorable terms that protect your investment, and configuring systems for seamless integration with your existing operations.

The Hidden Dangers of Traditional AI Selection
Most small business owners approach AI vendor selection backwards. They start with flashy demos, get dazzled by impressive features they'll never use, and make decisions based on what sounds good rather than what works. This approach leads to three common disasters that drain budgets and destroy confidence.

The Feature Trap catches entrepreneurs who believe more features equal better value. You'll see AI platforms boasting hundreds of capabilities, from natural language processing to predictive analytics to automated reporting. While these features sound impressive, they often create unnecessary complexity and higher costs. The reality? Most businesses use less than 20% of available features in any software platform.

The Demo Deception misleads business owners through carefully orchestrated presentations using perfect data scenarios. Vendors showcase their AI performing flawlessly with clean, organized information that rarely matches real-world business conditions. Your actual data—with its inconsistencies, gaps, and quirks—may perform dramatically differently than the polished demo suggests.

The Commitment Pressure forces premature decisions through limited-time offers and aggressive sales tactics. Vendors create artificial urgency, claiming special pricing expires soon or implementation slots are filling up quickly. This pressure leads to hasty decisions without proper evaluation, often resulting in solutions that don't match actual business needs.

The SHADOW Framework's Acquire step eliminates these traps through systematic evaluation that prioritizes business fit over vendor persuasion.

The Business-First Evaluation Framework

Your AI selection process must center on business impact, not technical specifications. This evaluation framework guides you through five critical assessment areas that determine long-term success.

Problem-Solution Alignment Assessment

Start by documenting your specific business challenge in precise terms. Don't just say "improve customer service"—define the exact problem: "reduce average response time from 4 hours to 30 minutes while maintaining quality." This specificity becomes your evaluation benchmark.

Create a **Problem Definition Matrix** that outlines:

Problem Element	Current State	Desired State	Success Metric
Response Time	4 hours average	30 minutes maximum	90% responses under 30 min
Quality Score	3.2/5 customer rating	4.5/5 customer rating	Monthly satisfaction surveys
Staff Productivity	15 tickets per day	25 tickets per day	Weekly performance tracking
Cost per Ticket	$12 average	$8 maximum	Monthly cost analysis

Each AI solution you evaluate must directly address these defined problems with measurable improvements. If a vendor can't clearly explain how their solution impacts your specific metrics, eliminate them immediately.

Implementation Complexity Analysis

Assess how easily each solution integrates with your existing systems and workflows. Complex implementations drain resources and create ongoing maintenance headaches that offset AI benefits.

The Integration Assessment Checklist:

[ ] **Data Requirements**: Does the solution work with your current data format, or does it require extensive data cleanup and restructuring?

[ ] **System Compatibility**: Will the AI solution integrate seamlessly with your existing software stack, or does it require expensive middleware or system changes?

[ ] **Training Demands**: How much time will your team need to become proficient with the new system? Count both initial training and ongoing skill development.

[ ] **Support Infrastructure**: What level of technical support does your team need to maintain optimal performance? Factor in both vendor support and internal resource requirements.

[ ] **Scalability Path**: How easily can the solution grow with your business? Consider both volume increases and feature expansion needs.

Vendor Stability and Support Evaluation

Your AI solution becomes part of your business infrastructure. Vendor reliability directly impacts your operational continuity and long-term success.

Financial Stability Indicators:

- Company funding history and current financial position
- Customer base size and growth trajectory
- Revenue diversification across market segments
- Investment backing and strategic partnerships

Support Quality Assessment:

- Response time commitments for different issue types
- Availability of phone, email, and chat support channels
- Escalation procedures for critical system failures
- Geographic support coverage matching your business hours

Product Development Commitment:

- Regular update and improvement schedules

- User feedback integration into product roadmap
- Investment in research and development
- Industry compliance and security updates

Request references from businesses similar to yours in size and industry. Speak directly with these customers about their experience, particularly regarding support responsiveness and problem resolution effectiveness.

Cost Structure and ROI Analysis

Understand the total cost of ownership beyond initial licensing fees. AI solutions often include hidden costs that significantly impact your return on investment.

Complete Cost Breakdown:

1. Initial Costs

- Software licensing or subscription fee
- Implementation and setup charge
- Data migration and integration expense
- Initial training and onboarding costs

2. Ongoing Expenses

- Monthly or annual subscription renewals
- Usage-based charges for processing volume
- Maintenance and support fees
- Additional user licenses as you scale

3. Hidden Costs

- Extra storage or bandwidth charges
- Premium feature access fees
- Custom development or configuration costs
- Training for new team members

4. Opportunity Costs

- Time invested in implementation and optimization
- Resources diverted from other business priorities
- Learning curve productivity impacts
- Potential switching costs if the solution doesn't work

Calculate ROI using conservative estimates that account for implementation delays and learning curves. Your projected benefits should exceed costs by at least 3:1 within the first year to justify the investment.

Security and Compliance Framework
Data security isn't optional—it's essential for business survival. Evaluate each vendor's security measures against your specific industry requirements and risk tolerance.

Security Assessment Areas:
- **Data Encryption**: Both in transit and at rest encryption standards
- **Access Controls**: User authentication and authorization protocols
- **Audit Trails**: Complete logging of system access and data modifications
- **Backup Systems**: Data recovery capabilities and disaster response plans
- **Compliance Certifications**: Industry-specific compliance standards (HIPAA, PCI-DSS, SOC 2)

Request detailed security documentation and don't accept vague assurances. Legitimate vendors provide comprehensive security information readily and transparently.

Negotiation Strategies for Maximum Protection
Once you've identified your preferred AI solution, strategic negotiation protects your investment and ensures vendor accountability. Small businesses often accept standard vendor terms without realizing their negotiating power. Every vendor wants your business, and you can secure favorable terms through informed negotiation.

Trial Period Negotiation
Never commit to an AI solution without extensive real-world testing. Demos show potential, but trials reveal actual performance with your data and workflows.

Essential Trial Elements:
- **Extended Timeline**: Request 30-60 day trials instead of standard 14-day periods. AI solutions require time to configure properly and evaluate thoroughly.
- **Full Feature Access**: Ensure trial access includes all features you're considering purchasing, not just basic functionality.
- **Data Integration**: Test with your actual business data, not vendor-provided sample datasets.
- **Support Inclusion**: Receive full implementation support during the trial period to

ensure proper setup and configuration.
- **Performance Guarantees**: Establish minimum performance benchmarks the solution must meet during the trial period.

Frame trial requests as essential for making an informed purchasing decision rather than seeking free service. Professional vendors understand that thorough evaluation leads to successful long-term partnerships.

Implementation Support Agreements

Secure comprehensive implementation support that ensures successful deployment without unexpected costs or delays.

Implementation Support Components:

- **Dedicated Implementation Specialist**: Assigned support person responsible for your successful deployment
- **Configuration Assistance**: Help setting up the system to match your specific business requirements
- **Data Migration Support**: Assistance transferring existing data into the new system
- **Integration Guidance**: Help connecting the AI solution with your existing software tools
- **Training Provision**: Comprehensive training for all team members who will use the system
- **Go-Live Support**: Extra attention during the initial deployment period to address immediate issues

Establish clear timelines and deliverables for each support element. Document vendor responsibilities and escalation procedures for addressing implementation challenges.

Performance and Service Level Agreements

Protect your business through contractual guarantees of system performance and vendor responsiveness.

Key Performance Metrics:

- **System Uptime**: Minimum 99.5% availability with compensation for extended outages
- **Response Speed**: Maximum processing times for typical AI operations
- **Accuracy Standards**: Minimum precision rates for AI predictions or recommenda-

tions

- **Support Response**: Maximum response times for different priority support requests

Service Level Protections:

- **Penalty Clauses**: Automatic credits or refunds for performance failures
- **Escalation Rights**: Direct access to senior technical resources for critical issues
- **Termination Rights**: Ability to cancel without penalty if performance standards aren't met
- **Data Portability**: Guaranteed ability to export your data if you need to switch vendors

Document all agreements in writing and ensure they're included in your final contract terms.

Pricing and Payment Terms

Negotiate pricing structures that align with your business model and cash flow requirements.

Favorable Payment Arrangements:

- **Performance-Based Pricing**: Link payments to achieved business outcomes rather than just system usage
- **Gradual Scale Pricing**: Start with lower rates that increase as you scale usage and prove value
- **Annual Payment Discounts**: Secure reduced rates for annual prepayments while maintaining termination rights
- **Usage Cap Protections**: Maximum monthly charges to prevent unexpected cost spikes during high-usage periods

Contract Protection Elements:

- **Price Lock Guarantees**: Fixed pricing for initial contract terms with controlled increase rates for renewals
- **Feature Grandfather Rights**: Continued access to current features even if vendor changes product offerings
- **Support Level Maintenance**: Guaranteed support quality levels throughout the contract period
- **Early Termination Rights**: Ability to cancel with reasonable notice if business needs change

Remember that initial vendor quotes often include substantial markup for negotiation. Professional vendors expect some back-and-forth discussion and respect businesses that understand their requirements clearly.

Configuration Best Practices for Seamless Integration

Proper configuration transforms a powerful AI solution into a seamless extension of your existing business operations. This phase determines whether your AI implementation enhances productivity or creates operational friction.

Data Integration Strategy

Your AI solution's effectiveness depends entirely on data quality and accessibility. Poor data integration creates bottlenecks that limit AI performance and frustrate users.

Data Preparation Framework:

1. Data Audit and Cleanup

- Identify all data sources the AI solution will access
- Remove duplicate records and inconsistent formatting
- Standardize naming conventions and data structures
- Fill critical data gaps that could impact AI accuracy

2. Integration Pathway Design

- Map data flow from source systems to AI platform
- Establish automated data synchronization schedules
- Create backup and recovery procedures for data protection
- Test integration pathways with sample data before full deployment

3. Data Quality Monitoring

- Implement ongoing data quality checks and alerts
- Establish procedures for handling data inconsistencies
- Create feedback loops for continuous data improvement
- Document data governance policies for team guidance

Common Integration Pitfalls to Avoid:

- **Data Silos**: Failing to connect all relevant data sources limits AI insights and recommendations
- **Format Inconsistencies**: Mixed data formats create processing errors and reduce accuracy

- **Update Delays**: Slow data synchronization creates AI recommendations based on outdated information
- **Access Restrictions**: Overly restrictive data permissions limit AI functionality and user productivity

Work closely with your vendor's technical team during data integration setup. Their experience with similar businesses provides valuable guidance for avoiding common configuration mistakes.

Workflow Optimization

Configure your AI solution to enhance existing workflows rather than replacing them entirely. Gradual integration reduces user resistance and maintains business continuity during the transition period.

Workflow Integration Approach:

1. Current Process Mapping

- Document existing workflows step-by-step
- Identify time-consuming manual tasks suitable for AI assistance
- Note decision points where AI insights could improve outcomes
- Recognize handoff points between team members or departments

2. AI Enhancement Design

- Determine where AI adds value without disrupting core processes
- Create parallel AI workflows that complement existing procedures
- Design fallback procedures for situations when AI recommendations aren't suitable
- Establish review points for monitoring AI impact on workflow efficiency

3. User Experience Optimization

- Minimize additional clicks or steps required to access AI features
- Integrate AI recommendations directly into existing software interfaces
- Provide clear explanations for AI suggestions to build user confidence
- Create shortcuts for frequently used AI functions

Team Transition Strategy:

- **Gradual Rollout**: Introduce AI features to small groups before company-wide deployment
- **Champion Development**: Identify early adopters who can help other team members

adapt
- **Feedback Collection**: Regular check-ins to identify and address user concerns quickly
- **Success Celebration**: Highlight early wins to build momentum and enthusiasm

Remember that workflow changes often face initial resistance. Focus on demonstrating clear benefits rather than mandating immediate adoption.

Performance Monitoring Setup

Establish comprehensive monitoring systems that track both AI performance and business impact from day one. Early monitoring identifies issues before they affect business operations and provides data for ongoing optimization.

Key Monitoring Categories:

1. Technical Performance Metrics
- System response times and processing speeds
- Error rates and failure patterns
- Resource utilization and capacity planning
- Integration stability and data synchronization

2. Business Impact Measurements
- Productivity improvements in targeted processes
- Cost reductions from automated tasks
- Quality improvements in output or decision-making
- Time savings for individual team members

3. User Adoption Tracking
- Feature usage rates and patterns
- User satisfaction scores and feedback
- Training completion and competency levels
- Support request volume and types

Monitoring Tool Configuration:

Create dashboards that provide real-time visibility into AI system performance and business impact. Include both automated alerts for technical issues and regular reports for management review.

Alert Framework

- **Critical Alerts**: System failures or security issues requiring immediate attention
- **Performance Warnings**: Degraded performance that could impact business operations
- **Usage Notifications**: Unusual usage patterns that might indicate problems or opportunities
- **Success Indicators**: Achievements of key performance targets or milestones

Document all monitoring procedures and ensure multiple team members understand how to interpret results and respond to alerts.

Security Configuration

Implement robust security measures that protect your business data while enabling AI functionality. Security configuration requires balancing access needs with protection requirements.

Security Implementation Checklist:

1. User Access Control

- Define role-based permissions for different team members
- Implement multi-factor authentication for system access
- Establish regular password update requirements
- Create procedures for adding and removing user access

2. Data Protection Measures

- Enable encryption for all data transmission and storage
- Configure automated backup systems with tested recovery procedures
- Implement access logging and audit trail maintenance
- Establish data retention and deletion policies

3. Network Security Setup

- Configure firewall rules for AI system access
- Implement VPN requirements for remote access
- Enable intrusion detection and prevention systems
- Establish secure communication channels with vendor support

Compliance Maintenance:

- **Regular Security Reviews**: Periodic assessment of security measures and access controls

- **Compliance Monitoring**: Ongoing verification of industry-specific regulatory requirements
- **Incident Response Planning**: Documented procedures for handling security breaches or data loss
- **Vendor Security Updates**: Process for implementing security patches and system updates

Involve your IT support team or consultant in security configuration to ensure all measures align with your existing infrastructure and policies.

The Acquire step of the SHADOW Framework eliminates the guesswork and risk from AI vendor selection. Through systematic evaluation focused on business fit rather than technical features, strategic negotiation that protects your investment, and thoughtful configuration that ensures seamless integration, you'll select and implement an AI solution that delivers immediate value while supporting long-term growth.

Your chosen AI solution now sits ready for deployment—the exciting phase where theory transforms into measurable business results. The Deploy step brings your carefully selected and configured AI system online through a parallel implementation that proves value without risking your existing operations.

CHAPTER NINE

DEPLOY - LAUNCHING YOUR PARALLEL SYSTEM

THE MOMENT OF TRUTH arrives when you press the button that changes everything. You've spent weeks preparing, researching, and planning, but now your AI solution goes from concept to reality in your actual business environment. This isn't a simulation or a test run on sample data—this is your AI working alongside your real operations, processing your actual transactions, and proving its worth in the most demanding laboratory of all: your daily business operations. The Deploy phase represents the bridge between preparation and proof, where months of careful planning crystallize into measurable results.

This chapter transforms AI deployment from a terrifying leap into a confident step forward.

The beauty of shadow deployment lies in its revolutionary approach to risk management. While your competitors agonize over the dangers of AI implementation, you'll be collecting real performance data from a system that can't possibly harm your operations. You're not replacing anything—you're adding intelligence. You're not risking disruption—you're creating opportunity. You're not gambling with your business—you're investing in its future with a safety net that eliminates every trace of implementation anxiety.

The Psychology of Deployment Fear

Before we dive into the technical aspects of launching your parallel AI system, we need to address the elephant in the room: deployment fear. Even with the safeguards of shadow implementation, many business owners experience a surge of anxiety when it's time to activate their AI solution. This fear is completely normal and stems from years of conditioning that equates business system changes with operational risk.

Traditional software implementations have trained us to expect disaster. We've all heard horror stories of companies that spent millions on systems that didn't work, databases that crashed, or integrations that brought operations to a standstill. These stories create a psychological barrier that makes any system deployment feel like Russian roulette with our business operations.

Shadow deployment eliminates this risk entirely. Your AI system operates in complete isolation from your production environment. It receives the same data your existing systems process, but it can't affect those systems in any way. Think of it like having a brilliant consultant watching your operations and taking notes, but never touching your actual processes. The consultant can observe, analyze, and provide insights, but they can't accidentally delete your customer database or crash your point-of-sale system.

This parallel approach creates what psychologists call a "safe learning environment." You get to experience the benefits of AI without the traditional risks, building confidence through positive experience rather than fear-based hesitation. Each day your shadow system runs successfully reinforces your decision to move forward with AI implementation.

Pre-Deployment Checklist

Before activating your shadow AI system, you need to complete a comprehensive pre-deployment checklist. This systematic approach ensures nothing falls through the cracks and your deployment proceeds smoothly from day one.

Technical Readiness Assessment:

[ ] **Data Integration Verification** - Confirm your AI system can access the data sources identified during the Harvest phase without interfering with existing data flows

[ ] **System Resource Check** - Verify your infrastructure can handle the additional processing load of running parallel systems

[ ] **Security Protocol Review** - Ensure your shadow system maintains the same security standards as your production environment

[ ] **Backup and Recovery Plan** - Document procedures for pausing or reverting the shadow system if unexpected issues arise

Operational Readiness Assessment:

[ ] **Staff Training Completion** - Confirm designated team members understand their roles in monitoring and managing the shadow system

[ ] **Communication Plan Activation** - Ensure all stakeholders know about the shadow deployment timeline and their responsibilities

[ ] **Performance Baseline Documentation** - Record current system performance metrics that will serve as comparison benchmarks

[ ] **Monitoring Dashboard Setup** - Configure real-time visibility into both existing operations and shadow system performance

Business Readiness Assessment:

[ ] **Budget Authorization** - Confirm all necessary funds are allocated and approved for the deployment period

[ ] **Timeline Alignment** - Verify the deployment schedule aligns with business cycles and doesn't conflict with critical operational periods

[ ] **Success Criteria Definition** - Establish clear, measurable goals that will determine deployment success

[ ] **Stakeholder Sign-off** - Obtain final approval from all decision-makers before activation

This checklist serves as your final safety net before deployment. Each item represents a potential failure point that could compromise your shadow implementation. By systematically addressing every element, you eliminate uncertainty and create confidence in your deployment process.

The Shadow Deployment Architecture

Understanding how your shadow system operates alongside existing operations is crucial for successful deployment. The architecture creates a sophisticated parallel processing environment that mirrors your production systems without interfering with them.

Data Flow Management:

Your shadow AI system receives identical data inputs as your production systems, but through completely separate channels. This is accomplished through data replication rather than data sharing. Your existing systems continue processing transactions exactly as they always have, while your shadow system processes copies of the same data simultaneously.

For example, if you're implementing AI for customer service ticket routing, your traditional routing system continues handling all incoming tickets normally. Simultaneously, your shadow AI system receives copies of the same tickets and processes them according to its algorithms. Both systems generate routing decisions, but only your existing system's decisions are implemented. The shadow system's decisions are recorded for comparison and analysis.

Processing Isolation:

The shadow system operates in complete isolation from your production environment. It has its own processing resources, its own data storage, and its own user interface. This isolation ensures that any issues with the shadow system—software bugs, configuration errors, or performance problems—cannot affect your existing operations.

This isolation extends to user access as well. Only designated team members have access to the shadow system interface. Your regular staff continue using existing systems exactly as they always have. They're completely unaware that a parallel AI system is operating alongside their familiar tools.

Performance Monitoring Integration:

While the shadow system operates independently, it integrates with your monitoring infrastructure to provide real-time visibility into comparative performance. Specialized dashboards display side-by-side metrics showing how your existing systems and shadow AI system handle identical workloads.

These dashboards become your window into AI performance, providing concrete data about processing speed, accuracy rates, and efficiency improvements. You'll watch in real-time as your AI system demonstrates its capabilities without any risk to your operations.

Step-by-Step Deployment Process

The deployment process follows a carefully orchestrated sequence designed to minimize risk while maximizing learning opportunities. Each step builds upon the previous one, creating a systematic progression from initial activation to full parallel operation.

Phase 1: Initial Activation (Days 1-3)

Your deployment begins with a soft launch focused on basic functionality verification.

During this phase, your shadow AI system processes a limited subset of data to ensure all connections work properly and baseline functionality operates as expected.

Start by activating your shadow system during off-peak hours when data volumes are lower and fewer people are available to notice any unexpected issues. Monitor system performance closely during these first few hours, watching for any signs of connectivity problems, processing errors, or resource conflicts.

The initial activation phase serves multiple purposes beyond technical verification. It builds your confidence in the deployment process, familiarizes your team with monitoring procedures, and establishes baseline performance metrics that will guide the remainder of your deployment.

Phase 2: Volume Scaling (Days 4-7)

Once basic functionality is confirmed, gradually increase the data volume processed by your shadow system. This scaling process reveals how your AI solution handles realistic workloads and identifies any performance bottlenecks before they become critical issues.

Monitor processing speeds, memory usage, and response times as data volumes increase. Compare these metrics against your existing system performance to quantify efficiency improvements. Document any issues that arise and work with your AI vendor to optimize performance before proceeding to full volume processing.

Volume scaling also reveals patterns in your AI system's decision-making processes. You'll begin to see how the AI handles different types of inputs, identifies edge cases that require human intervention, and adapts to variations in data quality or format.

Phase 3: Full Parallel Operation (Days 8-30)

With basic functionality confirmed and volume scaling completed, activate full parallel operation where your shadow AI system processes the same complete data set as your production systems. This phase provides the comprehensive performance data needed to make informed decisions about full integration.

During full parallel operation, your monitoring focus shifts from technical performance to business impact assessment. Track metrics like accuracy rates, processing speed improvements, error reduction, and efficiency gains. These business-focused metrics form the foundation of your ROI analysis and integration decision-making.

Full parallel operation also provides opportunities for staff training and change management preparation. Team members can observe AI decision-making processes, understand how the technology complements their existing skills, and prepare for the eventual transition to AI-enhanced operations.

Monitoring Protocols and Performance Tracking

Effective monitoring transforms deployment from a leap of faith into a data-driven decision process. Your monitoring protocols provide real-time visibility into system performance while building the evidence base needed to justify full AI integration.

Real-Time Performance Dashboards:

Create comprehensive dashboards that display side-by-side comparisons of your existing systems and shadow AI performance. These dashboards should include both technical metrics (processing speed, resource utilization, error rates) and business metrics (accuracy improvements, efficiency gains, cost savings).

Update dashboard displays in real-time to provide immediate feedback on AI performance. This immediate visibility builds confidence in the deployment process and enables rapid response to any issues that arise.

Design dashboard layouts for different audiences within your organization. Technical staff need detailed system performance data, while business leaders require high-level summaries focused on ROI and competitive advantage metrics. Create role-specific dashboard views that provide relevant information without overwhelming users with unnecessary detail.

Automated Alert Systems:

Configure automated alerts that notify relevant team members when performance thresholds are exceeded or unusual patterns are detected. These alerts serve as an early warning system that enables proactive issue resolution before problems impact business operations.

Alert thresholds should reflect your specific business requirements and risk tolerance. Set conservative thresholds initially, then adjust based on actual performance data as your deployment progresses. This approach ensures you catch potential issues early while avoiding alert fatigue from overly sensitive monitoring.

Performance Data Collection:

Systematic data collection during shadow deployment creates the evidence base needed for integration decision-making. Collect comprehensive data on processing accuracy, speed improvements, error reduction, and resource utilization.

Store performance data in formats that enable trend analysis and comparative reporting. This historical data becomes invaluable for optimizing AI performance and demonstrating ROI to stakeholders who weren't directly involved in the deployment process.

Staff Training and System Management

Successful shadow deployment requires your team to develop new skills while maintaining their existing responsibilities. The training approach must be practical, focused, and designed to build confidence rather than create additional stress.

Role-Specific Training Programs:

Different team members require different levels of AI system knowledge based on their responsibilities during shadow deployment. System administrators need deep technical knowledge, while business users need high-level understanding of AI capabilities and limitations.

Develop training programs tailored to specific roles within your organization. Technical staff need hands-on experience with system monitoring, troubleshooting, and performance optimization. Business users need conceptual understanding of how AI enhances their existing processes without replacing their expertise.

Create training materials that address common concerns and misconceptions about AI implementation. Many employees fear that AI will replace their jobs or make their skills obsolete. Address these concerns directly by demonstrating how AI enhances human capabilities rather than replacing them.

Monitoring Responsibilities:

Assign specific monitoring responsibilities to designated team members to ensure consistent oversight throughout the deployment period. These responsibilities should be clearly defined, documented, and integrated into existing job roles rather than creating additional workload burdens.

Primary monitors should have deep system knowledge and authority to make decisions about shadow system operation. Secondary monitors provide backup coverage and additional perspective on system performance. This redundancy ensures consistent monitoring coverage even when primary personnel are unavailable.

Communication Protocols:

Establish clear communication protocols for reporting issues, sharing performance insights, and coordinating system management activities. These protocols ensure information flows efficiently between technical staff, business users, and management throughout the deployment period.

Regular communication meetings keep all stakeholders informed about deployment progress and provide forums for addressing concerns or questions that arise. These meetings also serve as opportunities to celebrate early wins and build momentum for full AI integration.

Troubleshooting Common Deployment Issues

Even with careful planning and systematic deployment procedures, issues can arise during shadow implementation. Preparing for common problems and developing standard resolution procedures minimizes deployment disruption and maintains confidence in the AI implementation process.

Data Integration Challenges:

Data format inconsistencies, connectivity issues, and synchronization problems are the most common technical challenges during shadow deployment. These issues typically stem from differences between development environments and production systems that weren't apparent during initial testing.

Address data integration challenges through systematic diagnostic procedures that isolate and resolve specific problems. Work closely with your AI vendor's technical support team to leverage their experience with similar implementations and access to specialized troubleshooting tools.

Document all data integration issues and their resolutions to build institutional knowledge that will benefit future AI implementations. This documentation also provides valuable feedback to your AI vendor about real-world deployment challenges that may not be apparent in controlled testing environments.

Performance Optimization:

AI system performance often requires fine-tuning during deployment as the system adapts to actual data volumes, processing patterns, and business requirements. Performance optimization is an iterative process that continues throughout the shadow deployment period.

Monitor system performance continuously and make incremental adjustments based on observed behavior. Focus on optimizations that provide the greatest performance improvements with the least implementation complexity. Save more complex optimizations for later phases when basic functionality is stable and well-understood.

User Acceptance and Change Management:

Employee resistance to AI implementation can create deployment challenges even when the technology performs perfectly. Address user acceptance issues through transparent communication, hands-on training, and opportunities for staff to provide feedback about the AI implementation process.

Involve skeptical employees in monitoring and evaluation activities to help them understand AI capabilities and limitations firsthand. This direct experience often converts skeptics into advocates who become valuable champions for full AI integration.

Building Confidence Through Measurable Results

The ultimate goal of shadow deployment is building unshakeable confidence in your AI implementation through concrete, measurable results. This confidence comes from data, not faith—from proven performance, not vendor promises.

Quantifying Performance Improvements:

Track specific metrics that demonstrate AI value in terms your entire organization can understand. Focus on improvements in accuracy, speed, cost reduction, and customer satisfaction rather than technical performance metrics that may not resonate with business stakeholders.

Create before-and-after comparisons that clearly illustrate the impact of AI implementation on your business operations. These comparisons become powerful tools for building stakeholder support and justifying the investment in AI technology.

ROI Documentation:

Develop comprehensive ROI documentation that quantifies the business value of your AI implementation. Include both direct cost savings (reduced labor costs, improved efficiency) and indirect benefits (competitive advantages, improved customer satisfaction, enhanced decision-making capabilities).

ROI documentation serves multiple purposes beyond internal decision-making. It provides evidence for additional AI investments, demonstrates innovation leadership to customers and partners, and creates case studies that can be used for marketing and competitive positioning.

Success Story Development:

Document specific examples of how your AI system handled challenging situations, solved complex problems, or delivered unexpected insights. These success stories become powerful tools for building confidence in AI capabilities and generating enthusiasm for expanded implementation.

Success stories work because they translate abstract AI capabilities into concrete business benefits that everyone can understand. They demonstrate AI value in human terms rather than technical specifications, making the technology more accessible and less intimidating to skeptical stakeholders.

Preparing for Integration Success

Shadow deployment concludes with comprehensive preparation for full AI integration. This preparation phase ensures your transition from parallel operation to full implementation proceeds smoothly and delivers maximum business value.

Integration Planning:

Develop detailed integration plans that specify exactly how your proven AI system will replace or enhance existing processes. These plans should address technical integration requirements, staff training needs, change management procedures, and timeline considerations.

Integration planning requires close collaboration between technical staff, business users, and management to ensure all perspectives are considered and potential issues are identified before they become problems. The planning process itself builds organizational consensus and commitment to successful AI integration.

Performance Baseline Establishment:
Use shadow deployment performance data to establish realistic expectations for post-integration AI performance. These baselines become the foundation for ongoing performance monitoring and continuous improvement efforts after full integration.

Baseline establishment also provides objective criteria for determining integration success. Rather than relying on subjective impressions, you'll have concrete metrics that demonstrate whether your AI integration delivers promised benefits.

The Deploy phase represents the moment when AI transforms from concept to reality in your business environment. Through systematic shadow deployment, you've eliminated implementation risk while building unshakeable confidence in your AI solution's capabilities. Your parallel system has proven its worth through measurable results, documented performance improvements, and successful handling of real-world business challenges.

As you prepare to move beyond deployment into the Optimize phase, you're no longer hoping your AI investment will pay off—you're planning how to maximize returns that have already been proven. The shadow deployment data you've collected becomes the foundation for fine-tuning performance, optimizing efficiency, and building compelling business cases for expanded AI adoption throughout your organization.

CHAPTER TEN

OPTIMIZE - PROVING VALUE AND PERFORMANCE

RAW DATA TELLS STORIES, but only if you know how to listen. Your shadow AI system has been running for weeks now, quietly collecting performance metrics while your existing operations continue unchanged. But here's what separates successful AI adopters from those who abandon their efforts: they transform scattered data points into undeniable proof of competitive advantage. This optimization phase isn't just about making your AI work better—it's about building an iron-clad business case that makes full integration inevitable.

The difference between "trying AI" and "proving AI works" lies entirely in this chapter.

The Hidden Truth About AI Performance Data

Most business owners make a fatal mistake during their shadow implementation. They assume that because their AI system is "working," they've achieved success. They see improved processing times or reduced errors and think they're ready to move forward. This surface-level analysis leaves massive value on the table and creates weak business cases that fail when scrutinized by stakeholders or advisors.

The reality is that your shadow AI system generates multiple layers of performance data, each telling a different story about your competitive advantage. **Surface metrics** like processing speed or accuracy rates are just the beginning. **Operational metrics** reveal how AI impacts workflow efficiency, employee productivity, and resource allocation.

Business metrics uncover the true financial impact on revenue, costs, and profitability. **Strategic metrics** demonstrate how AI positions your business against competitors and opens new market opportunities.

Understanding these data layers transforms you from someone who "implemented AI" into someone who "proved AI delivers measurable business value." This distinction becomes crucial when you're ready to scale your AI adoption or when competitors start questioning your sudden operational advantages.

The Performance Analysis Framework

Your approach to analyzing AI performance data must be systematic and thorough. Random data collection leads to scattered insights that fail to build compelling narratives. The **Performance Analysis Framework** provides a structured methodology for extracting maximum value from your shadow implementation.

Step 1: Establish Your Baseline Reality

Before diving into AI performance metrics, you need crystal-clear documentation of your pre-AI baseline. This isn't just about recording numbers—it's about capturing the complete operational picture that AI will transform.

Document these baseline elements with precision:

- **Time Measurements**: Record exact minutes or hours required for each process step, including hidden time costs like setup, review, and correction activities
- **Quality Metrics**: Establish error rates, rework percentages, and customer satisfaction scores using specific, measurable criteria
- **Resource Consumption**: Track labor hours, material costs, and overhead expenses directly attributable to the process
- **Output Volume**: Measure daily, weekly, and monthly production capacity under current operations
- **Bottleneck Identification**: Map where delays occur, why they happen, and how frequently they disrupt workflow

Your baseline documentation serves as the foundation for every optimization decision. Without accurate baseline data, you can't prove improvement, justify investment, or demonstrate competitive advantage.

Step 2: Implement Comprehensive Data Collection

Your shadow AI system should capture performance data across multiple dimensions simultaneously. This multi-dimensional approach reveals optimization opportunities that single-metric analysis misses.

Operational Performance Metrics:

Metric Category	Key Measurements	Collection Frequency
Processing Speed	Task completion time, throughput rates	Real-time
Accuracy Rates	Error frequency, correction requirements	Daily
Resource Efficiency	CPU usage, memory consumption	Continuous
System Reliability	Uptime percentage, failure incidents	24/7 monitoring

Business Impact Metrics:

Impact Area	Measurement Focus	Reporting Schedule
Cost Reduction	Labor savings, material efficiency	Weekly
Revenue Enhancement	Increased capacity, improved quality	Monthly
Customer Experience	Response times, satisfaction scores	Ongoing
Competitive Position	Market response, advantage duration	Quarterly

Step 3: Conduct Comparative Analysis

Raw performance data becomes powerful when you compare AI results against your established baseline. This comparison reveals the true magnitude of your competitive advantage and identifies specific areas where optimization can multiply your returns.

Create side-by-side comparisons that highlight:

- **Speed Improvements**: Document percentage improvements in processing time, showing both average gains and best-case scenarios
- **Quality Enhancements**: Compare error rates, customer complaints, and rework requirements between AI and manual processes
- **Cost Reductions**: Calculate exact dollar savings in labor, materials, and overhead expenses
- **Capacity Increases**: Measure how AI enables higher output volumes without proportional resource increases

Advanced Optimization Strategies

Once you understand your AI system's current performance, you can implement targeted optimizations that maximize efficiency and ROI. These strategies go beyond basic parameter adjustments to unlock hidden value within your implementation.

Parameter Tuning for Maximum Impact

Your AI solution contains numerous adjustable parameters that influence performance outcomes. Most business owners accept default settings, missing opportunities for significant improvements. Systematic parameter optimization can double or triple your initial results.

Confidence Threshold Optimization:

AI systems use confidence scores to determine when they can handle tasks independently versus when they need human review. Adjusting these thresholds balances automation benefits with quality control:

- **Higher Thresholds** (85-95%): Fewer automated decisions but higher accuracy, suitable for critical processes where errors are costly
- **Lower Thresholds** (65-80%): More automated decisions with occasional review needs, ideal for high-volume, low-risk tasks
- **Dynamic Thresholds**: Adjust confidence requirements based on time of day, workload, or process complexity

Processing Speed Calibration: Most AI systems can be tuned for either speed or accuracy, depending on your business priorities:

- **Speed Optimization**: Reduce processing time by 20-40% while maintaining acceptable accuracy levels for time-sensitive operations
- **Accuracy Optimization**: Maximize precision for quality-critical processes where speed is secondary to perfection
- **Balanced Optimization**: Find the sweet spot that delivers optimal combinations of speed and accuracy for your specific use case

Resource Allocation Adjustment: Fine-tune how your AI system uses available computing resources to match your operational patterns:

- **Peak Performance Mode**: Allocate maximum resources during busy periods to handle increased workload
- **Efficiency Mode**: Reduce resource consumption during slower periods to minimize

operating costs

- **Predictive Scaling**: Automatically adjust resource allocation based on anticipated workload patterns

Workflow Integration Enhancement

The most significant optimization gains often come from improving how AI integrates with your existing workflows rather than improving the AI system itself. These integration enhancements can eliminate bottlenecks and create seamless operational flow.

Input Optimization:

Streamline how data flows into your AI system to reduce processing delays and improve accuracy:

- **Data Preprocessing**: Clean and format input data automatically to reduce AI processing time
- **Batch Processing**: Group similar tasks together to improve system efficiency and reduce overhead
- **Priority Queuing**: Process urgent tasks first while handling routine work during slower periods

Output Enhancement:

Optimize how AI results integrate back into your business processes:

- **Automated Routing**: Send AI outputs directly to the next process step without manual intervention
- **Quality Scoring**: Attach confidence indicators to AI results so staff know which outputs need additional review

Exception Handling: Create automatic protocols for managing cases where AI can't complete tasks successfully

Building Compelling Business Cases

Your optimization efforts generate the raw material for building business cases that make AI expansion inevitable. However, data alone doesn't create compelling narratives. You need to package your performance improvements into stories that resonate with stakeholders, advisors, and decision-makers.

The ROI Documentation Framework

Financial Impact Analysis:

Transform your performance data into clear financial statements that demonstrate AI's contribution to your bottom line:

- **Direct Cost Savings**: Calculate exact dollar amounts saved through reduced labor, materials, and overhead expenses
- **Revenue Enhancement**: Quantify additional revenue generated through increased capacity, improved quality, or faster customer service
- **Investment Recovery**: Document how quickly your AI investment pays for itself through operational improvements
- **Future Value Projection**: Estimate ongoing financial benefits over the next 12-24 months based on current performance trends

Competitive Advantage Documentation:

Demonstrate how your AI implementation creates sustainable advantages over competitors:

- **Speed Advantages**: Show how faster processing enables you to serve customers better or capture time-sensitive opportunities
- **Quality Differentiators**: Document how improved accuracy or consistency sets your business apart from competitors
- **Capacity Expansions**: Illustrate how AI enables you to handle larger projects or serve more customers without proportional cost increases
- **Innovation Positioning**: Position your AI adoption as evidence of forward-thinking leadership that attracts customers and talent

Risk Mitigation Evidence:

Address potential concerns by documenting how your AI implementation actually reduces business risks:

- **Consistency Improvements**: Show how AI eliminates human error and variability that previously created operational risks
- **Scalability Solutions**: Demonstrate how AI provides capacity expansion options that reduce growth-related risks
- **Knowledge Preservation**: Document how AI systems capture and preserve critical business knowledge that might otherwise be lost

- **Compliance Enhancement**: Illustrate how AI improves adherence to regulations, standards, or quality requirements

Creating Executive-Level Reports

Your optimization data needs to be presented in formats that busy executives and advisors can quickly understand and act upon. Executive-level reports focus on strategic implications rather than technical details.

The One-Page Success Summary

Create a single-page overview that captures your AI implementation's complete value story:

Implementation Overview:

Brief description of what AI solution you implemented and why:

- **Key Performance Improvements**: Top 3-5 metrics showing the most significant gains
- **Financial Impact**: Clear dollar amounts for cost savings and revenue enhancement
- **Competitive Advantages**: Specific ways AI positioning strengthens your market position
- **Next Steps**: Recommended actions for expanding or scaling your AI adoption

The 30-60-90 Day Projection

Use your optimization data to create realistic projections for continued AI benefits:

- **30 Days**: Immediate gains from full integration and initial optimization
- **60 Days**: Additional benefits from workflow refinements and staff adaptation
- **90 Days**: Compound advantages from operational efficiency and competitive positioning

The Expansion Roadmap

Document specific opportunities for applying your successful AI implementation to other business areas:

- **High-Priority Targets**: Processes similar to your current implementation that offer quick wins
- **Medium-Term Opportunities**: More complex applications that require additional planning but offer significant benefits
- **Strategic Initiatives**: Advanced AI applications that could transform your entire business model

Continuous Improvement Protocols

Optimization isn't a one-time activity—it's an ongoing process that ensures your AI implementation continues delivering increasing value over time. Establishing continuous improvement protocols maintains your competitive advantage and maximizes your AI investment.

Monthly Performance Reviews:

Schedule regular analysis sessions to identify new optimization opportunities:

- **Trend Analysis**: Look for patterns in performance data that suggest adjustment opportunities
- **Bottleneck Identification**: Find new constraints that limit AI effectiveness as your business evolves
- **Enhancement Testing**: Try small modifications to parameters or workflows to test improvement potential

Quarterly Strategy Updates:

Use performance data to guide strategic decisions about AI expansion and business development:

- **ROI Reassessment**: Update financial projections based on actual performance trends
- **Competitive Analysis**: Evaluate how your AI advantages compare to competitor developments
- **Expansion Planning**: Identify the most promising areas for additional AI implementation

Annual Value Audits:

Conduct comprehensive reviews of your AI implementation's total business impact:

- **Strategic Value Assessment**: Measure how AI has changed your competitive position and growth trajectory
- **Investment Analysis**: Calculate total return on AI investment including both direct and indirect benefits
- **Future Planning**: Develop long-term strategies for maintaining and expanding your AI advantages

As you complete your optimization work and build compelling documentation of your AI success, you'll notice something remarkable happening: your confidence in AI implementation grows exponentially. The data you've collected doesn't just prove your AI works—it proves you can make AI work. This confidence becomes the foundation for seamlessly integrating your proven AI solution into full operations, where it transforms from an experiment into the competitive advantage that drives your business forward.

The next chapter reveals how to transition from shadow implementation to full integration without disrupting your operations or risking the success you've already achieved. You'll discover the precise methods for weaving your optimized AI solution into the fabric of your business, creating sustainable competitive advantages that compound over time.

Chapter Eleven

Weave - Seamless Integration Mastery

The moment of truth arrives when shadow becomes reality. Your AI solution has proven its worth in parallel testing, delivering measurable results that exceed expectations and validate your investment. Now comes the final step that separates successful AI implementations from expensive experiments—weaving your proven technology seamlessly into your business operations without missing a beat. This integration phase determines whether your 60-day AI journey becomes a permanent competitive advantage or just another costly lesson learned.

The Integration Imperative

Most small business owners assume that successful testing automatically guarantees smooth integration, but this couldn't be further from the truth. Statistics reveal a sobering reality: while 78% of shadow AI implementations prove successful during testing phases, only 34% achieve seamless operational integration without significant disruption. The difference lies not in the technology itself, but in the strategic approach to transitioning from parallel testing to full deployment.

Your shadow system has been running quietly alongside your existing processes, proving its value while protecting your operations from risk. But now it's time to make the switch—to replace your old process with your new AI-powered workflow. This transition requires the same methodical approach that made your shadow implementation successful, combined with change management strategies specifically designed for small business environments.

The stakes couldn't be higher. A poorly executed integration can undo months of progress, create employee resistance that lasts for years, and damage customer relationships you've spent decades building. But when done correctly, integration becomes the moment your business truly awakens to its AI-powered potential.

Understanding the Integration Mindset

Before we explore the tactical elements of seamless integration, you need to understand the psychological shift that must occur within your organization. Integration isn't just a technical process—it's a human transformation that requires careful orchestration of emotions, expectations, and operational realities.

Your team has watched your shadow implementation with a mixture of curiosity and concern. Some employees have embraced the technology enthusiastically, seeing it as a tool that makes their jobs easier and more interesting. Others remain skeptical, worried about job security or convinced that the AI system will create more problems than it solves. Still others fall somewhere in between, cautiously optimistic but uncertain about what full implementation means for their daily routines.

This range of reactions is completely normal and actually healthy for your organization. It demonstrates that your team is thinking critically about the changes ahead and considering the implications for their work. Your job during integration is to channel this energy productively, addressing concerns while building excitement for the improved workflows that await.

The key insight here is that successful integration happens in hearts and minds before it happens in systems and processes. When your team understands the "why" behind the change and feels confident about their role in the new workflow, technical integration becomes surprisingly straightforward. When they don't, even the most elegant technical solution will face resistance that undermines its effectiveness.

Strategic Transition Planning

The foundation of seamless integration lies in meticulous transition planning that accounts for every aspect of your operation. This isn't about creating elaborate project management charts or complex timelines—it's about thinking through the practical realities of switching from your current process to your AI-enhanced workflow while maintaining business continuity.

Timing Your Cutover

The timing of your integration matters more than most business owners realize. You want to choose a period when your business can absorb temporary inefficiencies without significant customer impact. For retail businesses, this might mean avoiding holiday seasons or major sale periods. For service businesses, it could mean scheduling integration during traditionally slower periods when staff has more bandwidth to adapt to new processes.

Consider creating a transition timeline that spans 2-3 weeks rather than attempting a single-day cutover. This approach allows you to migrate different aspects of your process gradually, reducing risk while giving your team time to adapt to each change before introducing the next one.

Parallel Operation Strategy

During your transition period, you'll run both your old process and your new AI-enhanced workflow simultaneously. This might seem inefficient, but it provides crucial safety nets that protect your business from integration risks. If problems arise with the AI system, you can immediately fall back to your proven process while troubleshooting issues.

This parallel operation also gives your team confidence that they're not jumping off a cliff without a safety net. Knowing they can return to familiar processes if needed reduces anxiety and makes them more willing to embrace the new workflow.

Customer Communication Planning

Your customers don't need to know about your internal process changes, but they should experience the benefits without any service disruption. Develop communication strategies that highlight improvements they'll notice—faster response times, more accurate information, or enhanced service capabilities—without getting into technical details about your AI implementation.

Prepare your customer-facing team with simple explanations for any questions that might arise. Most customers appreciate businesses that invest in better service, so frame your integration as part of your commitment to continuous improvement rather than a risky technology experiment.

Building Your Integration Team

Successful integration requires a small but dedicated team of internal champions who can guide the transition process. This team doesn't need to be large—in most small businesses, 2-4 people can effectively manage the entire integration—but they need to be strategically chosen based on their influence, technical comfort, and communication skills.

Selecting Your Champions

Your integration team should include one person from management who can make decisions quickly, one employee who will use the AI system regularly and can speak to its practical benefits, and one person who's naturally good at helping others learn new processes. If your business allows, also include someone who was initially skeptical about the AI implementation but has come around after seeing the shadow system results.

This diverse team brings different perspectives and communication styles that help address the full range of employee concerns and learning preferences. The former skeptic is particularly valuable because they can speak authentically about overcoming initial reservations—something that carries more weight with hesitant employees than management enthusiasm alone.

Training Your Trainers

Before your integration team can help others adapt to the new process, they need to become genuine experts in the AI-enhanced workflow. This means spending significant time with the shadow system, understanding not just how to use it but why it works the way it does and how to troubleshoot common issues.

Your team champions should practice explaining the new process to others, developing simple analogies and step-by-step instructions that make sense to people with different learning styles. They should also prepare for common questions and concerns, armed with specific examples and data from your shadow implementation that demonstrate the system's benefits.

Comprehensive Staff Training Protocols

The quality of your staff training directly impacts the success of your integration. Poor training creates frustrated employees who resist the new system, while excellent training builds enthusiastic adopters who help others embrace the change. The secret lies in designing training that addresses both technical skills and emotional concerns simultaneously.

Phased Learning Approach

Rather than overwhelming your team with comprehensive training sessions, break learning into digestible phases that build confidence progressively. Start with basic concepts and simple tasks, allowing people to experience early wins that build their comfort with the AI system. Then gradually introduce more advanced features and complex workflows as their confidence grows.

This phased approach works particularly well for small businesses where employees wear multiple hats and can't spend entire days in training sessions. Short, focused training modules that people can complete between other responsibilities ensure better retention and less disruption to daily operations.

Hands-On Practice Sessions

Nothing builds confidence like hands-on experience with the actual system they'll be using. Design practice sessions using real data from your business so employees can see exactly how the AI system will impact their specific responsibilities. This practical approach helps people understand not just what to do, but why the new process is better than the old one.

Create scenarios based on common situations your team encounters, allowing them to work through the AI-enhanced workflow in a safe environment where mistakes don't have real consequences. This practice time is invaluable for building the muscle memory and confidence needed for smooth daily operations.

Addressing Resistance Constructively

Some employees will embrace the new system immediately, while others will need more time and support to feel comfortable with the change. Recognize that resistance often stems from legitimate concerns rather than simple stubbornness, and address these concerns directly rather than dismissing them.

Common concerns include worries about job security, fear of making mistakes with new technology, and skepticism about whether the AI system will actually make their work easier. Address each concern with specific information about how the implementation will impact individual roles, emphasizing ways the AI system enhances rather than replaces human judgment and expertise.

Common Concern	Effective Response Strategy
"Will this replace my job?"	Show how AI handles routine tasks, freeing them for higher-value work
"What if I break something?"	Demonstrate built-in safeguards and reversible actions
"This seems complicated"	Start with simple tasks and build complexity gradually
"The old way works fine"	Share specific metrics showing AI improvements
"I'm not good with technology"	Pair them with tech-comfortable colleagues for support

Advanced Monitoring and Performance Systems

Once your AI system transitions from shadow to full operation, your monitoring needs become more sophisticated. You're no longer just tracking performance to prove value—you're monitoring to ensure sustained success, identify optimization opportunities, and catch potential issues before they impact your business.

Real-Time Performance Dashboards

Establish monitoring systems that give you immediate visibility into how your AI solution is performing compared to your baseline metrics. These dashboards should track key performance indicators that matter to your business—processing speed, accuracy rates, customer satisfaction scores, or cost savings—in real-time format that allows quick decision-making.

Your monitoring system doesn't need to be complex or expensive. Many AI solutions include built-in analytics capabilities, and simple spreadsheet-based tracking can be effective for smaller implementations. The key is choosing metrics that truly reflect business impact rather than technical statistics that don't translate to operational value.

Automated Alert Systems

Configure alerts that notify you when performance metrics fall outside acceptable ranges or when unusual patterns emerge that might indicate problems. These early warning systems help you address issues proactively rather than discovering problems after they've already impacted your operations or customers.

Set alert thresholds based on your shadow implementation data, allowing for normal variations while flagging significant deviations that require attention. Remember that some fluctuation is normal as your team adapts to new workflows, so avoid setting alerts so sensitive that they create false alarms.

Continuous Optimization Protocols

Your AI system's performance will evolve as your team becomes more proficient and as the system processes more data from your business. Establish regular review cycles—weekly for the first month, then monthly thereafter—to analyze performance trends and identify opportunities for improvement.

These optimization sessions should involve your integration team and key users who can provide insights into how the system performs in daily practice. Look for patterns in user behavior, common points of confusion, and workflows that could be streamlined further. The goal is continuous improvement rather than perfection, building on the strong foundation your shadow implementation provided.

Managing the Transition Experience

The days and weeks following your cutover from shadow to full implementation are critical for long-term success. During this period, your team is adapting to new routines while you're monitoring system performance and customer impact. How you manage this transition experience shapes whether your AI implementation becomes a permanent competitive advantage or a source of ongoing frustration.

Daily Check-ins and Support

For the first two weeks following integration, conduct brief daily check-ins with team members who use the AI system regularly. These don't need to be formal meetings—quick conversations at the start of shifts or informal touchpoints throughout the day work well for small businesses. The goal is to identify issues quickly while they're still small and manageable.

During these check-ins, ask specific questions about what's working well and what's causing frustration. More importantly, listen for signs that people are developing workarounds or reverting to old processes when they encounter difficulties. These behaviors indicate training gaps or system configuration issues that need immediate attention.

Rapid Response Problem-Solving

When issues arise during the transition period, respond quickly and decisively. Problems that linger for days or weeks create lasting negative impressions and undermine confidence in the new system. Even if you can't solve every problem immediately, acknowledge concerns promptly and communicate your plan for addressing them.

Keep a running log of issues and resolutions during your transition period. This documentation helps you identify patterns that might indicate broader training needs or system adjustments. It also provides valuable reference material for future AI implementations as you scale your success to other business processes.

Celebrating Early Wins

Don't wait until your integration is complete to acknowledge successes. Celebrate early wins and improvements as they occur, helping your team see tangible benefits from their efforts to adapt to new processes. These celebrations don't need to be elaborate—simple recognition of improved metrics or positive customer feedback can be powerful motivators.

Share specific examples of how the AI system is delivering on its promises, using real data from your business rather than hypothetical benefits. When employees see concrete evidence that their extra effort during the transition is paying off, they're more likely to maintain enthusiasm for ongoing optimization and improvement.

Building Long-Term Success Habits

The ultimate goal of your integration process isn't just to get your AI system running smoothly—it's to establish the organizational habits and capabilities that support ongoing AI success. This means creating systems for continuous improvement, developing internal expertise, and building the cultural foundation for future AI implementations.

Knowledge Transfer and Documentation

As your team becomes proficient with the AI system, capture their learning and insights in documentation that can support future team members and additional AI implementations. This isn't about creating complex technical manuals, but rather practical guides that reflect real-world experience with your specific business processes.

Encourage your most experienced users to mentor new employees, creating knowledge transfer systems that don't depend entirely on formal training programs. This peer-to-peer learning often proves more effective than top-down instruction because it addresses practical questions and concerns from people who've actually worked through the same challenges.

Performance Culture Development

Your AI implementation success creates an opportunity to strengthen your organization's focus on data-driven decision making and continuous improvement. Use the metrics and insights from your AI system to reinforce the value of measuring performance and optimizing processes based on evidence rather than assumptions.

This cultural shift pays dividends beyond your current AI implementation, creating organizational capabilities that support future technology adoption and business improvement initiatives. Teams that become comfortable with performance tracking and optimization develop competitive advantages that extend far beyond any single AI solution.

Preparing for What's Next

Your successful integration of your first AI solution marks the end of one journey and the beginning of another. You've proven that your business can adopt AI technology safely and profitably, building internal capabilities and confidence that position you for ongoing AI expansion. The question now becomes: where do you go from here?

Scaling Success Patterns

The methodical approach that made your first AI implementation successful can be replicated for future projects with even greater efficiency. You now have internal champions who understand AI implementation, proven training methods that work for your team, and monitoring systems that can be adapted for new applications.

More importantly, you've overcome the psychological barriers that prevent most small businesses from adopting AI technology. Your team has experienced firsthand that AI can make their work easier and more interesting rather than threatening their job security. This mindset shift makes future implementations significantly easier to plan and execute.

Building Strategic Advantage

Your AI-powered operations give you competitive advantages that compound over time. While competitors struggle with implementation fears and analysis paralysis, you're already optimizing your AI-enhanced processes and identifying opportunities for additional automation and intelligence.

The data your AI system generates provides insights that can inform strategic decisions about everything from staffing and inventory to customer service and marketing. These insights, combined with your growing AI expertise, position your business to capitalize on opportunities that less tech-savvy competitors can't even recognize.

The transformation from shadow to full AI implementation represents more than a technological upgrade—it's the moment your business truly awakens to its AI-powered potential. You've successfully navigated the integration process that stops most small businesses in their tracks, proving that sophisticated AI capabilities are within reach of any determined entrepreneur willing to start before they feel completely ready.

As you move forward into Part III, you'll discover how to leverage your AI success for maximum competitive positioning and business growth. Your first AI victory lap awaits, and with it, the recognition and advantages that come from being among the first in your industry to crack the code of profitable AI implementation.

You've made it this far, and I hope you're enjoying the book and finding valuable insights. If you have found even one piece of information helpful, your fellow readers would love to hear about it.

Why Your Review Matters:

- Helps others find reliable information
- Guides the development of future books and resources
- Contributes to a community of like-minded readers

Leave Your Review in 60 Seconds: Simply click or scan the QR code below to leave your review on Amazon. It only takes a minute, but your influence could last a lifetime.

Part III: Acceleration

Rivanna Heights Media

Chapter Twelve

Your First AI Victory Lap

Your first AI success just became your most powerful marketing weapon. This moment represents far more than operational improvement—it's your golden ticket to industry leadership and accelerated business growth. Most business owners celebrate quietly in their office, missing the enormous opportunity to turn their AI breakthrough into sustained competitive advantage. But you're about to discover how to transform this single victory into an unstoppable momentum engine that positions your company as the innovative leader others desperately want to emulate.

The Hidden Value of Your Achievement

You've just accomplished something that 87% of small businesses are still afraid to attempt. While your competitors debate whether AI is worth the risk, you've proven it works. While they analyze case studies from Fortune 500 companies, you've created your own success story. While they wait for perfect certainty, you've built real competitive advantage.

This achievement carries exponentially more value than the immediate operational benefits you're experiencing. Your willingness to start before feeling ready has positioned you months—sometimes years—ahead of businesses still trapped in research mode. That head start becomes your moat, but only if you leverage it correctly.

The mistake most business owners make is treating their AI implementation like an internal process improvement. They quietly enjoy the benefits while keeping their success story locked away from the market. This approach wastes the most valuable asset they've created: proof that they're innovative leaders who can execute when others hesitate.

Quantifying Your Success Story

Your AI implementation generated specific, measurable results that tell a compelling story. These numbers become the foundation for everything that follows—your marketing messages, your competitive positioning, and your expansion strategy.

Document the Complete Transformation

Start by capturing every aspect of your AI-driven improvement. Your documentation needs to tell a complete before-and-after story that demonstrates clear value creation.

Time savings represent your most relatable metric. Calculate the exact hours your AI solution saves weekly, then project that across months and years. If your AI implementation saves 8 hours per week, that's 416 hours annually—equivalent to hiring a part-time employee without salary, benefits, or management overhead.

Cost reduction provides immediate ROI justification. Track every expense your AI solution eliminated or reduced. This includes direct costs like processing fees, but also hidden expenses like error correction, rework, and opportunity costs from delayed responses.

Revenue impact often surprises business owners with its magnitude. AI implementations frequently generate revenue through faster customer response times, improved accuracy, or enhanced service capabilities. A customer service AI that reduces response time from 4 hours to 15 minutes doesn't just save money—it wins business from competitors who can't match that speed.

Quality improvements create long-term competitive advantages. Document accuracy improvements, consistency gains, and error reductions. These metrics become especially powerful when you can show how they translate into customer satisfaction or retention improvements.

Create Compelling Comparison Tables

Visual representations of your improvement make your success story instantly understandable. Create tables that show before-and-after metrics across key performance indicators.

Metric	Before AI	After AI	Improvement
Processing Time	45 minutes	3 minutes	93% reduction
Error Rate	8%	0.5%	94% improvement
Customer Response Time	4 hours	15 minutes	96% reduction
Weekly Labor Hours	20 hours	2 hours	90% reduction
Monthly Cost	$3,200	$1,400	56% reduction

These numbers tell a story that's impossible to ignore. They demonstrate not just improvement, but transformation. When prospects see these results, they don't question whether AI works—they question whether they can afford to fall further behind.

Building Your Innovation Narrative

Your AI success story needs to position you as the forward-thinking leader who saw opportunity where others saw risk. This narrative becomes a powerful differentiator that sets you apart from competitors still debating whether to act.

Craft Your Pioneer Positioning

Position yourself as the business owner who recognized AI's potential before it became obvious. Your story isn't about being the smartest person in the room—it's about being the most decisive. While others analyzed, you implemented. While others worried, you succeeded.

This positioning works because it addresses a fundamental truth about innovation adoption. Early movers don't necessarily have better technology or larger budgets. They have better judgment about when to act despite uncertainty. That judgment becomes a competitive advantage that extends far beyond your AI implementation.

Your narrative should emphasize the strategic thinking behind your decision. You didn't implement AI because it was trendy. You implemented it because you recognized that competitive timing matters more than perfect preparation. This perspective demonstrates strategic leadership that customers, partners, and industry peers respect.

Document Your Implementation Journey

Your implementation story becomes a powerful case study that demonstrates your company's execution capabilities. This story shows that you don't just talk about innovation—you deliver results.

Share the specific challenges you overcame during implementation. These details make your story credible and relatable. Other business owners facing similar challenges see that you've navigated the path successfully.

Highlight the strategic decisions that led to success. Explain why you chose your specific AI solution, how you managed the implementation process, and what you learned along the way. This information positions you as a knowledgeable resource others can trust.

Include lessons learned that could help others avoid common pitfalls. This generous sharing of knowledge establishes thought leadership while demonstrating confidence in your competitive position. You're so far ahead that helping others won't threaten your advantage.

Converting Success Into Market Position

Your AI implementation proves something powerful to your market: you're the kind of business that gets things done while others make excuses. This proof becomes a magnet for customers who want to work with innovative, forward-thinking companies.

Leverage Success for Customer Acquisition

Customers increasingly prefer working with businesses that demonstrate innovation leadership. Your AI implementation provides concrete evidence that you're ahead of the curve, not behind it. This positioning attracts customers who value efficiency, reliability, and cutting-edge service.

Use your AI success story in sales conversations to differentiate yourself from competitors. When prospects compare vendors, your proven ability to implement AI solutions demonstrates operational sophistication that competitors can't match. You're not promising future improvements—you're delivering current advantages.

Create marketing materials that highlight your AI-powered capabilities without getting technical. Focus on the customer benefits: faster service, higher accuracy, more reliable delivery. These benefits matter more to customers than the technical details of how you achieve them.

Position for Premium Pricing

AI-powered efficiency often justifies premium pricing because customers receive superior value. Your implementation allows you to deliver better results faster, which typically commands higher prices in competitive markets.

Calculate the value you deliver to customers through your AI enhancements. If your AI allows you to deliver projects 40% faster with 90% fewer errors, that additional value justifies pricing premiums. Customers pay more for better results, and your AI implementation delivers measurably better results.

Document customer feedback about your improved service levels. Testimonials that specifically mention speed, accuracy, or reliability improvements provide social proof that your AI investment creates real customer value. These testimonials become powerful sales tools that justify your positioning.

Scaling Your Success

Your first AI victory proves that you can successfully implement AI solutions. This proof removes the uncertainty barrier that prevented additional AI investments. Now you can scale confidently because you've demonstrated the ability to execute successfully.

Identify Next Implementation Opportunities

Use your success to evaluate additional AI opportunities with confidence. You now understand the implementation process, vendor selection criteria, and success factors. This knowledge dramatically reduces the risk and complexity of subsequent implementations.

Look for processes that share characteristics with your successful implementation. Similar complexity levels, data requirements, and integration needs increase the likelihood of similar success. Your proven methodology applies most effectively to comparable situations.

Consider customer-facing applications that could amplify your competitive advantage. While your first implementation might have focused on internal efficiency, customer-facing AI applications create visible differentiation that's harder for competitors to ignore or match.

Build Internal AI Expertise

Your successful implementation creates internal knowledge that becomes increasingly valuable as you scale. The team members who managed your first AI project now possess practical experience that's rare in small business environments.

Document the processes and decision-making frameworks that led to success. This documentation becomes a playbook for future implementations, reducing learning curves and increasing success probability.

Consider designating an internal AI champion who takes ownership of expanding your AI capabilities. This person becomes your internal expert who can evaluate new opportunities, manage vendor relationships, and oversee implementations.

Creating Industry Influence

Your AI success positions you to become an influential voice in your industry. This influence creates business development opportunities, partnership possibilities, and thought leadership positioning that drives long-term growth.

Share Your Knowledge Strategically

Speaking about your AI implementation at industry events positions you as an innovation leader. These speaking opportunities create visibility, credibility, and business development prospects that extend far beyond your immediate market.

Write articles or case studies about your implementation experience. Industry publications frequently seek real-world AI success stories from small businesses. Your content reaches potential customers, partners, and industry influencers.

Participate in industry discussions about AI adoption. Your practical experience gives you credibility that theoretical knowledge can't match. This participation builds your reputation as a knowledgeable resource others trust.

Mentor Other Business Owners

Helping other business owners navigate AI implementation builds relationships while establishing your expertise. This mentoring creates goodwill, networking opportunities, and potential partnership possibilities.

Consider offering consulting services based on your implementation experience. Other businesses will pay for guidance from someone who's successfully navigated the process they're contemplating.

Join or create industry groups focused on AI adoption. Your leadership in these groups positions you at the center of innovation discussions while building valuable business relationships.

Building Momentum for Continuous Innovation

Your AI success creates momentum that makes future innovation initiatives easier to justify and implement. This momentum becomes a sustainable competitive advantage that compounds over time.

Establish Innovation as Core Identity

Position innovation as a fundamental characteristic of your business culture. Your AI implementation provides evidence that innovation isn't just talk—it's how you operate. This positioning attracts customers, employees, and partners who value forward-thinking approaches.

Create internal processes that systematically evaluate new technology opportunities. Your proven ability to implement AI successfully reduces resistance to future innovation initiatives.

Budget specifically for innovation projects. Your AI ROI justifies dedicated innovation spending that allows you to maintain your competitive edge through continuous improvement.

Prepare for Industry Evolution

Your early AI adoption positions you to adapt quickly as technology evolves. While competitors struggle with their first AI implementations, you'll be ready for advanced applications that create even greater competitive advantages.

Stay connected with AI vendors and technology partners. Your status as a successful implementer gives you early access to new capabilities and beta programs that could provide additional competitive edges.

Monitor your industry for signs that AI adoption is accelerating. Your head start becomes more valuable as adoption increases because the gap between early adopters and late adopters widens over time.

The foundation you've built through your first AI success extends far beyond operational improvement. You've proven your ability to execute when others hesitate, created measurable competitive advantages, and positioned yourself as an industry leader. This positioning becomes the platform for sustained growth, premium pricing, and market leadership that your competitors will struggle to match.

Your victory lap isn't just celebration—it's preparation for the next phase of your business evolution. The confidence, credibility, and competitive advantage you've built through AI implementation become the foundation for achieving business goals that seemed impossible just months ago.

Now that you've experienced the power of strategic AI implementation and positioned yourself as an industry innovator, you're ready to scale these successes across your entire operation. The next chapter reveals how to systematically identify and prioritize your next AI implementation opportunities, building on your proven success to create comprehensive competitive advantages that compound over time.

Chapter Thirteen

Scaling Beyond Your First Win

Your first AI victory is a stepping stone, not your destination.

Success in AI isn't about achieving one breakthrough and calling it done. It's about building momentum that carries you forward into bigger wins, greater efficiency, and competitive advantages that compound over time. That first implementation you just completed? It's given you something far more valuable than cost savings or time reduction—it's given you proof that you can succeed with AI, and more importantly, a proven blueprint for doing it again.

Your journey from AI skeptic to AI implementer has equipped you with the most powerful asset any small business can have in today's market: demonstrated capability combined with systematic methodology.

The Strategic Framework for Identifying Your Next AI Opportunities

Most business owners make a critical mistake after their first AI success. They celebrate the win, enjoy the benefits, and then... wait. They wait for the next obvious opportunity to present itself, or they assume they need to start completely from scratch when considering their next AI project. This passive approach wastes the momentum you've built and allows competitors to close the gap you've worked so hard to create.

Your first AI implementation has given you something invaluable: **data about your business's AI readiness**. You now know exactly how your team responds to new technology, which vendors deliver on their promises, what implementation challenges are real versus imagined, and most importantly, where the highest ROI opportunities exist within your specific business model.

The strategic framework for identifying your next opportunities isn't about starting over—it's about **pattern recognition and strategic expansion**. You're not looking for completely new territory to conquer; you're looking for adjacent processes that share similar characteristics to your successful implementation.

Start with process similarity analysis. Your first AI success solved a specific type of business challenge, whether it was automating repetitive tasks, improving decision-making speed, enhancing customer interactions, or increasing data accuracy. The fastest path to your second win is finding other processes in your business that share these same fundamental characteristics.

Create a **business process inventory** using this proven methodology:

1. **Map every recurring process** in your business that takes more than 30 minutes per week
2. **Categorize each process** by type: data processing, customer communication, decision-making, monitoring, or creative tasks
3. **Rate each process** on effort required (1-10) and business impact potential (1-10)
4. **Identify processes that match your first AI success pattern** in terms of data availability, task repetition, and success metrics

Your second AI implementation should score high on impact potential while sharing DNA with your first success. This approach reduces implementation risk while maximizing your chances of achieving similar or better results.

Leverage your vendor relationships strategically. The AI provider you worked with for your first implementation has insight into your business operations, team dynamics, and success patterns that no other vendor possesses. They've seen you succeed, and they want you to succeed again because your success validates their solution and creates a case study for future clients.

Schedule a **strategic expansion consultation** with your current vendor. Come prepared with your process inventory and specific questions about where their technology could deliver similar results. Many AI vendors offer existing clients preferential pricing for additional implementations because the integration overhead is significantly lower.

Don't limit yourself to your current vendor, but use them as your starting point. They may have complementary solutions you haven't considered, or they may honestly tell you that another vendor would be better suited for specific use cases. This transparency actually strengthens your relationship and positions you as a sophisticated buyer for future implementations.

Prioritization Methods Using Your Proven Success Patterns

Random AI implementation leads to random results. Strategic AI implementation leads to predictable competitive advantages. Your first success has revealed patterns about what works in your business environment, and these patterns become your decision-making framework for future investments.

The ROI-proven prioritization matrix takes the guesswork out of choosing your next AI project. This isn't theoretical—it's based on real data from your actual implementation experience.

Evaluation Criteria	Weight	Scoring Method
Similarity to First Success	30%	Rate 1-10 based on process type, data requirements, and team involvement
Revenue Impact Potential	25%	Calculate potential revenue increase or cost reduction within 90 days
Implementation Complexity	20%	Rate 1-10 based on technical requirements and operational changes needed
Team Readiness	15%	Rate 1-10 based on staff availability and change management requirements
Competitive Advantage	10%	Rate 1-10 based on how visible this improvement would be to customers

Score each potential AI project using this matrix, with higher scores indicating higher priority. But here's the key insight most businesses miss: **always choose the project that scores highest on similarity to your first success**, even if another project scores higher overall. Why? Because your second AI implementation needs to build confidence and momentum, not test your limits.

Your third and fourth implementations can be more adventurous. Your second implementation should be a confidence builder that proves your success wasn't a fluke and establishes you as someone who "gets" AI implementation. This psychological momentum is far more valuable than the marginal difference between project ROI calculations.

Use the 90-day rule for prioritization. Any AI project that can't demonstrate measurable improvement within 90 days should be postponed until you've achieved three successful implementations. This rule keeps you focused on wins that build momentum rather than moonshot projects that could undermine confidence.

Create implementation waves, not implementation chaos. Group potential projects into waves based on resource requirements and complexity:
- **Wave 1**: Projects similar to your first success that require minimal new learning
- **Wave 2**: Projects that expand into adjacent business areas using proven methodologies
- **Wave 3**: Projects that require new vendor relationships or significantly different approaches

Complete all Wave 1 projects before moving to Wave 2. This approach ensures each success builds naturally on the previous one, creating a compounding effect that makes each subsequent implementation easier and more likely to succeed.

Building Internal AI Expertise and Capabilities

Your first AI implementation succeeded because you followed a proven methodology, but your future AI implementations will succeed because you've built internal capability that makes AI adoption feel natural rather than disruptive. The difference between businesses that implement one AI solution and businesses that become AI-powered organizations lies in their approach to building internal expertise.

Designate your AI champion, don't assume they'll emerge naturally. Every successful AI scaling effort has one person who becomes the internal expert, advocate, and go-to resource for AI-related questions and decisions. This person doesn't need to be your most technical employee—they need to be your most AI-curious employee who has demonstrated the ability to learn new systems and communicate complex ideas to others.

Your AI champion's responsibilities expand beyond managing current implementations:
- **Vendor relationship management**: Serving as the primary contact for all AI vendors and staying current on product updates and new capabilities
- **Opportunity identification**: Regularly auditing business processes to identify new AI implementation opportunities using your established criteria

- **Team training and support**: Helping other employees adapt to AI-enhanced processes and addressing concerns or resistance
- **Performance monitoring**: Tracking ROI and success metrics across all AI implementations and identifying optimization opportunities
- **Industry intelligence**: Staying informed about AI trends and competitive activities in your industry

Invest in formal AI education for your champion. This doesn't mean sending them back to school for a computer science degree—it means providing them with structured learning opportunities that build practical AI implementation skills.

Budget $2,000-$5,000 annually for your AI champion's education. This investment might include:
- **Industry-specific AI conferences** that focus on practical implementation rather than theoretical research
- **Vendor training programs** that deepen expertise in your current AI solutions and related technologies
- **Online certification programs** from recognized organizations that validate AI implementation skills
- **Mastermind groups or peer networks** where they can learn from other businesses' AI implementation experiences

Create AI implementation documentation that scales with your growth. Your first AI implementation probably generated some documentation, but scaling requires systematic knowledge capture that makes future implementations faster and more reliable.

Develop these essential documentation assets:
- **Implementation playbooks** that capture step-by-step processes for different types of AI projects
- **Vendor evaluation templates** that standardize how you assess new AI solutions
- **ROI calculation worksheets** that ensure consistent financial analysis across all projects
- **Change management protocols** that help your team adapt to new AI-enhanced processes
- **Performance monitoring dashboards** that track success metrics across all AI implementations

Build AI fluency across your entire team, not just your AI champion. The goal isn't to make everyone an AI expert—it's to make everyone comfortable with AI as a business tool. This cultural shift is what separates businesses that scale AI successfully from those that struggle with adoption.

Implement monthly **AI awareness sessions** where your team learns about:
- How current AI implementations are improving business results
- Upcoming AI projects and how they'll affect different roles
- AI basics that help employees understand what's happening "behind the scenes"
- Success stories from other small businesses using similar AI solutions

These sessions should be brief (15-20 minutes), practical (focused on your actual implementations), and encouraging (celebrating wins and addressing concerns). The goal is building comfort and enthusiasm, not technical expertise.

Scaling Through Strategic Vendor Partnerships

Your relationship with AI vendors changes dramatically after your first successful implementation. You're no longer a prospective customer who might succeed—you're a proven customer who has succeeded. This shift in status opens doors to opportunities and partnerships that weren't available when you were just researching AI solutions.

Leverage your success story for better terms and access. AI vendors need case studies and reference customers almost as much as you need their technology. Your successful implementation has value to them beyond your monthly subscription fee, and you should use this value strategically.

Request these advantages based on your proven success:
- **Preferential pricing for additional implementations** or volume discounts for multiple solutions
- **Beta access to new features** that could provide competitive advantages before they're widely available
- **Direct access to product development teams** for feature requests that align with your business needs
- **Marketing partnership opportunities** that position your business as an AI leader in your industry
- **Priority technical support** and implementation assistance for future projects

Diversify your vendor relationships strategically, not randomly. Your first AI success proves you can work effectively with at least one AI vendor, but scaling requires relationships with multiple vendors who specialize in different business functions.

Develop a **vendor portfolio strategy** that balances specialization with integration:
- **Primary vendor**: Your first successful vendor who becomes your go-to partner for similar implementations
- **Complementary vendors**: 2-3 additional vendors whose solutions integrate well with your primary vendor and cover different business functions
- **Emerging vendors**: 1-2 newer companies whose innovative solutions could provide competitive advantages, even if they're riskier

Create vendor accountability through performance partnerships. As you scale your AI implementations, shift from transactional vendor relationships to performance-based partnerships where vendors have financial incentives to ensure your success.

Negotiate contracts that include:
- **Success milestones** with bonus payments for achieving specific ROI targets
- **Performance guarantees** with penalty clauses for solutions that don't meet agreed-upon metrics
- **Implementation support commitments** that ensure adequate resources for successful deployment
- **Integration responsibilities** that hold vendors accountable for working well with your existing systems

Measuring and Communicating Your AI Transformation

Scaling AI successfully requires more than just implementing additional solutions—it requires building a compelling narrative about your business transformation that motivates your team, impresses your customers, and intimidates your competitors. The measurements and communication strategies you develop become powerful assets for business growth beyond just operational improvement.

Develop AI transformation metrics that tell your story. Traditional business metrics capture individual improvements, but they don't capture the compound effect of multiple AI implementations working together. You need new metrics that showcase your evolution from traditional business to AI-powered organization.

Track these transformation indicators:

Metric Category	Specific Measurements	Business Impact
Process Efficiency	Time saved per week across all AI implementations	Demonstrates operational improvement
Decision Speed	Reduction in time from data gathering to decision-making	Shows competitive responsiveness
Customer Experience	Improvement in response times, accuracy, and satisfaction	Proves customer value creation
Team Productivity	Increase in high-value work time versus administrative tasks	Highlights human potential unleashing
Innovation Capacity	Number of new capabilities or services enabled by AI	Demonstrates strategic advantage

Create monthly AI transformation reports that communicate progress to your team, customers, and industry contacts. These reports shouldn't be technical documents—they should be compelling stories about business evolution and competitive positioning.

Your monthly reports should include:
- **AI wins of the month**: Specific examples of how AI implementations solved problems or created opportunities
- **Productivity improvements**: Quantified time savings and efficiency gains across the organization
- **Customer impact stories**: Examples of how AI enhancements improved customer experiences or outcomes
- **Team empowerment examples**: Stories of how AI freed employees to focus on more meaningful, strategic work
- **Competitive positioning updates**: Information about how your AI capabilities compare to industry standards

Use your AI transformation for market positioning and business development. Your systematic approach to AI implementation becomes a powerful differentiator in sales conversations, partnership discussions, and industry networking. Customers increasingly want to work with businesses that are innovative and efficient, and your AI adoption demonstrates both.

Develop **AI-enhanced service offerings** that leverage your implementations to create new revenue streams:
- **Faster turnaround times** enabled by AI automation that justify premium pricing
- **Enhanced accuracy and quality** powered by AI analysis that reduces customer risk

- **New service capabilities** that weren't economically feasible before AI implementation
- **Predictive insights and recommendations** that add strategic value beyond basic service delivery

Position yourself as an AI thought leader in your industry. Your systematic approach to AI scaling gives you unique insights that other business owners desperately need. Sharing these insights builds your reputation, creates networking opportunities, and often leads to unexpected business opportunities.

Share your AI journey through:
- **Industry association presentations** about practical AI implementation for small businesses
- **Local business group discussions** where you can mentor other entrepreneurs considering AI adoption
- **Social media content** that showcases your AI-enhanced capabilities and results
- **Customer newsletters** that highlight how AI improvements benefit their experience and outcomes

Creating Your AI Implementation Calendar

Random AI implementations create random results and random stress. Strategic AI implementations create predictable competitive advantages and manageable change. The difference lies in having a systematic calendar that sequences your AI projects for maximum success and minimal disruption.

Plan your AI implementations in quarterly waves that align with your business cycles and resource availability. This approach ensures each implementation gets adequate attention while preventing AI initiatives from overwhelming your operational responsibilities.

Quarter 1: Consolidation and optimization

Focus on maximizing the value of your existing AI implementations before adding new ones. This quarter is about proving that your first success wasn't a fluke and building confidence for more ambitious projects.

Activities for Quarter 1:
- **Performance analysis** of your first AI implementation with detailed ROI documentation

- **Process refinement** to eliminate remaining inefficiencies and maximize automation benefits
- **Team training enhancement** to ensure everyone is fully comfortable with AI-enhanced processes
- **Vendor relationship optimization** to negotiate better terms and explore additional capabilities

Quarter 2: Adjacent expansion

Implement AI solutions in business areas that are closely related to your first success. This approach leverages your existing knowledge and vendor relationships while extending AI benefits to new processes.

Activities for Quarter 2:

- **Similar process identification** using your proven evaluation criteria
- **Implementation of one new AI solution** that shares characteristics with your first success
- **Cross-training initiatives** that spread AI expertise across more team members
- **Documentation updates** that capture lessons learned and best practices

Quarter 3: Strategic diversification

Expand into different types of AI applications that address different business functions. This quarter is about broadening your AI capabilities and exploring new competitive advantages.

Activities for Quarter 3:

- **New vendor evaluation** for AI solutions in different business areas
- **Implementation of AI solution** in a different functional area (if first was operations-focused, try customer-facing)
- **Industry benchmark analysis** to ensure your AI adoption pace maintains competitive advantages
- **Customer communication strategy** to highlight your AI-enhanced capabilities

Quarter 4: Integration and scaling preparation

Focus on making all your AI implementations work together seamlessly and preparing for more aggressive scaling in the following year.

Activities for Quarter 4:
- **System integration projects** that connect different AI solutions for compound benefits
- **Annual ROI analysis** that quantifies your total AI transformation impact
- **Next year planning** that identifies opportunities for more ambitious AI projects
- **Team capability assessment** that determines training needs for advanced AI implementations

Avoiding Common Scaling Pitfalls

Scaling AI implementations successfully requires learning from the mistakes of businesses that attempted similar journeys but failed to achieve sustainable competitive advantages. These pitfalls are predictable and preventable, but only if you're aware of them and actively working to avoid them.

Pitfall #1: The "shiny object" syndrome

After experiencing success with your first AI implementation, you'll be bombarded with vendors, articles, and conference presentations about amazing new AI capabilities. The temptation to chase every new AI trend rather than systematically building on your proven success can derail your scaling efforts.

Solution: Stick to your prioritization matrix and quarterly planning calendar. New AI opportunities should be evaluated against your established criteria, not implemented because they seem interesting or cutting-edge.

Pitfall #2: Underestimating change management requirements

Your first AI implementation probably required some team adaptation, but scaling AI across multiple business processes requires systematic change management that addresses cumulative resistance and change fatigue.

Solution: Budget 20% of each new AI implementation timeline for change management activities. This includes team training, process adjustment, and addressing concerns that arise as AI becomes more prevalent in daily operations.

Pitfall #3: Neglecting vendor relationship management

As you work with multiple AI vendors, the complexity of managing different contracts, support relationships, and integration requirements can become overwhelming without systematic approach.

Solution: Assign vendor relationship management responsibility to your AI champion and create standardized processes for contract management, performance monitoring, and integration coordination.

Pitfall #4: Focusing on technology instead of business outcomes
The excitement of AI capabilities can shift attention from business results to technical features. This focus leads to implementations that are technically impressive but don't deliver meaningful competitive advantages.

Solution: Maintain strict adherence to ROI requirements and business outcome measurements. Every AI implementation should deliver measurable business improvements within 90 days, regardless of how impressive the technology might be.

Your journey from single AI implementation to AI-powered organization represents more than operational improvement—it represents business evolution that positions you as a leader in your industry. The systematic approach you're developing now will serve as the foundation for sustained competitive advantages that compound over time, creating gaps between your capabilities and your competitors' that become increasingly difficult for them to close.

The next chapter will show you how to apply this scaling methodology specifically to customer experience improvements, where AI can create the most visible and impactful competitive advantages that customers notice immediately and competitors struggle to replicate.

Chapter Fourteen

The Customer Experience Revolution

AI doesn't just automate processes—it creates customer experiences that build empires. When you think about the businesses that dominate their industries, they all share one common trait: they've figured out how to make every customer interaction feel personal, immediate, and valuable. What used to require massive teams and enterprise-level budgets is now within reach of any small business owner willing to think differently about customer experience. The companies that understand this shift aren't just surviving—they're thriving while their competitors wonder what happened.

Your customers don't care about your business size, your budget constraints, or your technical limitations. They care about one thing: how you make them feel when they interact with your business. And here's the reality that's going to either excite or terrify you—AI has fundamentally changed what customers expect from every business interaction, regardless of company size.

The Hidden Customer Experience Arms Race

Right now, while you're reading this, your competitors are testing AI solutions that could fundamentally change how customers experience your industry. This isn't some distant future scenario—it's happening today in businesses just like yours.

Take Sarah's boutique marketing agency in Denver. Six months ago, she was manually responding to client inquiries, scheduling follow-ups in a paper planner, and losing potential customers because she couldn't respond fast enough outside business hours. Today, her AI-powered customer experience system handles initial inquiries instantly, schedules consultations automatically, and even provides personalized service recommendations based on each prospect's specific needs.

The result? Her conversion rate from inquiry to client increased by 230%, and she's booking consultations while sleeping. But here's what really matters—her clients consistently tell her that working with her agency feels more professional and responsive than working with much larger competitors.

The Customer Experience Gap

Most small business owners focus on delivering their core service or product exceptionally well, which is absolutely necessary. But they're missing the bigger picture. Today's customers expect:

- **Instant responses** to inquiries, regardless of time or day
- **Personalized recommendations** based on their specific needs and history
- **Proactive communication** about issues before they become problems
- **Seamless experiences** across all touchpoints with your business
- **Predictive service** that anticipates their needs

These expectations aren't unreasonable—they're the new baseline. Companies like Amazon, Netflix, and Spotify have trained customers to expect these experiences everywhere, not just from tech giants.

Applying SHADOW Framework to Customer-Facing AI Implementation

The beauty of the SHADOW Framework is that it works perfectly for customer experience improvements because you can test everything without disrupting your current customer service approach. Let me show you exactly how this works.

Screen: Identifying Your Customer Experience Goldmine

The first step is finding where AI can create the biggest impact on customer satisfaction with the lowest implementation risk. Most small business owners make the mistake of trying to revolutionize everything at once. That's a recipe for overwhelm and failure.

Instead, you want to identify the **single customer touchpoint** where improvement would create the most dramatic result. Here's how to find it:

The Customer Journey Audit

Map out every interaction a customer has with your business, from first awareness to post-purchase follow-up. For each touchpoint, ask these three questions:

1. What frustrates customers most at this stage?

2. What would delight them if it worked perfectly?

3. How much time does this currently consume for you or your team?

The sweet spot is where high customer frustration meets high time consumption for your team. This is where AI can create the most dramatic improvement for both you and your customers.

Common High-Impact Customer Touchpoints:

Touchpoint	Customer Frustration	AI Solution Potential	Implementation Difficulty
Initial Inquiry Response	Waiting hours/days for responses	Instant, personalized responses	Low
Appointment Scheduling	Phone tag, limited availability visibility	24/7 automated scheduling	Low
Order Status Updates	Having to call for updates	Proactive status notifications	Medium
Product Recommendations	Generic suggestions	Personalized recommendations	Medium
Support Issue Resolution	Repeating information, long wait times	Intelligent routing and context	High

Real-World Example: Mike's HVAC Success

Mike runs a small HVAC business in Phoenix. His customer journey audit revealed that emergency service calls were his biggest opportunity. Customers were frustrated because they couldn't reach him after hours, and he was losing thousands in emergency service revenue.

Using the SHADOW Framework, Mike implemented an AI phone system that handles after-hours calls. The system qualifies the emergency level, schedules appropriate service windows, and even provides basic troubleshooting for simple issues.

The result? His emergency service revenue increased 180% in the first quarter, and his customer satisfaction scores jumped from 7.2 to 9.1 out of 10. More importantly, he's sleeping better because customers feel heard and helped, even when he's not available.

Harvest: Gathering Customer Data and Resources

Once you've identified your target touchpoint, you need to gather the resources necessary for successful implementation. This isn't about collecting massive amounts of data—it's about collecting the **right** data efficiently.

Essential Customer Data Collection:

1. Historical interaction data - How long do responses typically take? What are the most common questions? What time of day do most inquiries arrive?

2. Customer preference data - How do your best customers prefer to communicate? What information do they need to feel confident in their decisions?

3. Current process documentation - How does your team currently handle these interactions? What works well? What consistently causes problems?

Building Internal Support

Customer experience improvements affect everyone on your team, so you need buy-in from the start. The key is showing how AI will make their jobs easier, not replace them.

Frame the conversation around **enhancement, not replacement**:

- "This will handle the routine questions so you can focus on the complex customer needs that really matter"
- "You'll have more time to build relationships instead of answering the same questions repeatedly"
- "Customers will get faster responses, which means they'll be happier when they talk to you"

Budget Planning for Customer Experience AI

Most customer experience AI solutions for small businesses range from $50-$500 per month, depending on complexity and volume. The key is starting with a solution that can grow with you.

Budget considerations:

- **Initial setup costs** (usually one-time)
- **Monthly subscription fees** (typically based on usage)
- **Integration costs** (often minimal with modern solutions)
- **Training time investment** (usually 5-10 hours total)

Acquire: Selecting Your Customer Experience AI Solution

The customer experience AI market is filled with options, which can feel overwhelming. But when you focus on your specific use case, the choice becomes much clearer.

Vendor Evaluation Framework for Customer Experience AI

Criteria	Weight	Questions to Ask
Ease of Integration	30%	Can this work with our current systems? How long is setup?
Customization Options	25%	Can we train it on our specific business? Does it sound like us?
Scalability	20%	Can it grow as our business grows? What are the usage limits?
Support Quality	15%	How quickly do they respond? Do they understand small business needs?
Cost Structure	10%	Is pricing predictable? Are there hidden fees?

Popular Customer Experience AI Categories

- **Chatbots and Virtual Assistants** - Handle initial inquiries, provide basic information, route complex questions to humans
- **Automated Scheduling Systems** - Allow customers to book appointments 24/7, reduce phone tag, sync with your calendar
- **Personalized Recommendation Engines** - Suggest products or services based on customer history and preferences
- **Proactive Communication Systems** - Send updates, reminders, and follow-ups automatically based on customer behavior

Configuration Best Practices

Once you've selected your solution, proper configuration is crucial for success. Here's what matters most:

- **Train the AI with your actual customer language** - Use real emails, chat logs, and phone transcripts to train the system
- **Set clear escalation rules** - Define exactly when the AI should hand off to a human
- **Customize the personality** - Make sure the AI sounds like your brand, not like a robot
- **Test with friendly customers first** - Get feedback before full deployment

Deploy: Launching Your Parallel Customer Experience System

This is where the Shadow Framework really shines for customer experience improvements. You can test your AI solution alongside your existing process without any risk to customer satisfaction.

Parallel Deployment Strategy:

1. **Route 10% of interactions to the AI system** while handling the rest manually
2. **Monitor both systems simultaneously** to compare performance

3. **Gradually increase AI handling** as confidence and performance improve
4. **Maintain human backup** for all AI interactions during testing

30-Day Deployment Timeline:

Week 1: Soft Launch

- Route only internal test interactions through AI
- Team members test all major scenarios
- Refine responses based on team feedback

Week 2: Friendly Customer Testing

- Route 5% of real customer interactions to AI
- Monitor every AI interaction closely
- Collect customer feedback actively

Week 3: Expanded Testing

- Increase to 15% of customer interactions
- Begin measuring performance metrics
- Adjust AI responses based on real customer feedback

Week 4: Performance Evaluation

- Route 25% of interactions through AI
- Complete comprehensive performance analysis
- Prepare for optimization phase

Staff Training for Customer Experience AI

Your team needs to understand how to work **with** AI, not just how to use it. This includes:

- **When to intervene** in AI conversations
- **How to seamlessly take over** from the AI system
- **What to do** when the AI makes mistakes
- **How to improve** the AI based on customer feedback

Optimize: Proving Value and Improving Performance

The optimization phase is where you turn your customer experience AI from "pretty good" to "absolutely amazing." This requires systematic analysis and continuous improvement.

Key Customer Experience Metrics to Track:

Metric	Measurement Method	Target Improvement
Response Time	Average time from inquiry to first response	75% reduction
Customer Satisfaction	Post-interaction surveys (1-10 scale)	15% increase
Conversion Rate	Inquiries that become customers	25% increase
Resolution Rate	Issues resolved without human intervention	60% of routine issues
Revenue per Customer	Average purchase value	20% increase

Data Analysis Techniques for Customer Experience

- **Conversation Quality Analysis** - Review AI interactions weekly to identify improvement opportunities
- **Customer Sentiment Tracking** - Use feedback tools to understand how customers feel about AI interactions
- **Performance Comparison** - Compare AI-handled interactions to human-handled ones
- **Revenue Impact Measurement** - Track how AI interactions affect sales and customer lifetime value

Real-World Optimization Example: Lisa's Online Store

Lisa runs a specialty food business online. After implementing her customer experience AI, she noticed that while response times improved dramatically, conversion rates weren't increasing as expected.

Through conversation analysis, she discovered that the AI was providing accurate information but wasn't creating emotional connection with customers. She refined the AI's responses to include more personal touches and product stories.

The result? Conversion rates increased 40% within two weeks of the optimization. Customers started commenting that her business felt more personal and engaging than larger competitors.

Fine-Tuning Strategies:

- **A/B test different response styles** to find what resonates with your customers
- **Adjust AI personality** based on customer feedback and brand alignment

- **Optimize handoff triggers** to ensure complex issues reach humans quickly
- **Personalize responses** based on customer history and preferences

Weave: Seamless Integration Into Full Operations

The final step is transitioning from shadow implementation to full operational integration. This is where your customer experience transformation becomes permanent and scalable.

Integration Planning Checklist:

[ ] All team members trained on new AI-enhanced process

[ ] Backup procedures established for AI system failures

[ ] Customer communication plan for the transition

[ ] Performance monitoring systems in place

[ ] Escalation procedures refined and tested

Change Management for Customer Experience Teams

Your team might feel nervous about relying more heavily on AI for customer interactions. Address these concerns directly:

- **Share success metrics** from the shadow implementation phase
- **Highlight positive customer feedback** about AI interactions
- **Emphasize how AI improves their effectiveness**, not replaces them
- **Provide ongoing training** as the system evolves

Monitoring Systems for Sustained Performance

Once fully integrated, you need systems to ensure your customer experience AI continues performing well:

1. **Daily performance dashboards** showing key metrics
2. **Weekly conversation reviews** to catch quality issues early
3. **Monthly customer feedback analysis** to identify improvement opportunities
4. **Quarterly system updates** to maintain competitive advantage

Case Studies: Small Businesses Winning with Customer Experience AI

Let me share three detailed case studies that show exactly how small businesses are using customer experience AI to compete with much larger companies.

Case Study 1: David's Auto Repair Shop

David owns a three-bay auto repair shop in suburban Atlanta. His biggest challenge was managing customer communication throughout the repair process. Customers constantly called for updates, and his mechanics were interrupted dozens of times per day.

SHADOW Implementation:

Screen: Identified customer communication during repairs as the highest-impact opportunity

Harvest: Collected historical repair data and common customer questions

Acquire: Selected an AI system that integrates with his garage management software

Deploy: Ran the AI system parallel to manual updates for 30 days

Optimize: Refined AI responses based on customer feedback and reduced false information

Weave: Fully integrated the system with automated photo updates and completion notifications

Results:

Customer satisfaction increased from 6.8 to 9.2 out of 10

Phone interruptions decreased by 85%

Mechanic productivity increased 20%

Customer referrals increased 150%

Average repair ticket increased $75 due to better communication about recommended services

Case Study 2: Jennifer's Consulting Practice

Jennifer runs a small business consulting practice specializing in retail strategy. Her challenge was qualifying prospects and scheduling initial consultations efficiently.

SHADOW Implementation:

Screen: Focus on prospect qualification and consultation scheduling

Harvest: Analyzed successful client patterns and common qualifying questions

Acquire: Implemented AI chatbot with scheduling integration

Deploy: Tested with 20% of website visitors while maintaining manual process

Optimize: Refined qualifying questions based on actual client success patterns

Weave: Fully automated prospect qualification and scheduling

Results:

Consultation booking rate increased 180%

Qualified prospect percentage increased from 45% to 78%

Time spent on initial prospect calls decreased 60%

Revenue per consultation increased 35% due to better qualification

Client acquisition cost decreased $400 per client

Case Study 3: Mark's E-commerce Business

Mark sells outdoor gear through his online store. His challenge was providing personalized product recommendations that matched customer needs and preferences.

SHADOW Implementation:

Screen: Identified product recommendation as the highest-impact opportunity

Harvest: Analyzed purchase history, browsing behavior, and return patterns

Acquire: Selected AI recommendation engine with e-commerce integration

Deploy: Tested recommendations for 25% of customers while maintaining manual approach

Optimize: Refined recommendation algorithms based on purchase and return data

Weave: Implemented personalized recommendations across all customer touchpoints

Results:

Average order value increased 45%

Customer retention rate increased 60%

Product return rate decreased 30%

Customer lifetime value increased $180

Email marketing click-through rates increased 120%

Advanced Strategies for AI-Powered Customer Insights and Personalization

Once you've successfully implemented your first customer experience AI solution, you can begin exploring more sophisticated strategies that create truly differentiated customer experiences.

Predictive Customer Behavior Analysis

Advanced AI can predict customer needs before they express them. This includes:

- **Purchase timing predictions** - Knowing when customers are likely to need your services again

- **Churn risk identification** - Recognizing customers who might leave before they decide to
- **Upsell opportunity detection** - Finding the perfect moment to offer additional services
- **Seasonal behavior patterns** - Understanding how customer needs change throughout the year

Hyper-Personalization Techniques

Move beyond basic personalization to create experiences that feel individually crafted:

- **Dynamic content adaptation** - Website and email content that changes based on individual customer preferences
- **Personalized pricing strategies** - Offering promotions and discounts based on individual customer value and behavior
- **Customized communication timing** - Reaching customers when they're most likely to engage
- **Individual customer journey optimization** - Adapting the entire customer experience based on personal preferences and history

Creating Competitive Moats Through Customer Experience

The ultimate goal is creating customer experiences so good that competitors can't easily replicate them. This happens when you:

- **Combine multiple AI systems** to create seamless, integrated experiences
- **Build proprietary data advantages** through consistent customer interaction and feedback
- **Develop unique service offerings** that leverage your AI capabilities
- **Create switching costs** through personalized experiences that customers don't want to lose

The ROI of Customer Experience AI

Let's talk numbers because ultimately, your customer experience improvements need to drive business results. The businesses that successfully implement customer experience AI typically see returns across multiple areas.

Direct Revenue Impact:

Business Type	Average Conversion Rate Increase	Average Order Value Increase	Customer Retention Improvement
Service Businesses	35-60%	N/A	40-70%
E-commerce	25-45%	20-35%	50-80%
Professional Services	50-85%	15-25%	60-90%
Local Retail	30-50%	25-40%	45-65%

Cost Reduction Benefits:

- **Reduced customer service costs** - AI handles 60-80% of routine inquiries
- **Improved operational efficiency** - Less time spent on repetitive customer communications
- **Lower customer acquisition costs** - Better customer experiences drive more referrals
- **Decreased churn costs** - Proactive AI communication prevents customer loss

Competitive Positioning Value:

The hardest benefit to quantify but often the most valuable is the competitive positioning advantage. When your customer experience significantly exceeds expectations for your business size, you:

- **Command premium pricing** because customers perceive higher value
- **Win against larger competitors** in head-to-head comparisons
- **Generate organic marketing** through customer word-of-mouth
- **Attract higher-quality customers** who value excellent service

Common Pitfalls and How to Avoid Them

Even with the SHADOW Framework, some small business owners make mistakes that limit their customer experience AI success. Here are the most common pitfalls and how to avoid them.

Pitfall 1: Over-Automating Too Quickly

Many business owners get excited about AI capabilities and try to automate everything immediately. This creates robotic experiences that customers hate.

Solution: Always maintain human options and gradually increase automation based on customer feedback and comfort levels.

Pitfall 2: Ignoring Brand Personality
AI systems often sound generic unless specifically trained to match your brand voice and personality.

Solution: Spend time training your AI system to communicate in your brand's unique voice. Use actual customer conversations as training examples.

Pitfall 3: Not Measuring the Right Metrics
Some business owners focus only on efficiency metrics (response time, cost reduction) while ignoring customer satisfaction and business impact.

Solution: Always balance efficiency metrics with customer satisfaction and revenue impact measurements.

Pitfall 4: Insufficient Team Training
Teams that don't understand how to work with AI systems often create disconnected customer experiences.

Solution: Invest in comprehensive team training that covers both technical operation and customer experience principles.

Pitfall 5: Static Implementation
Setting up customer experience AI and never improving it leads to stagnant results and eventually declining performance.

Solution: Establish regular review and optimization schedules to continuously improve performance based on customer feedback and business results.

Scaling Your Customer Experience Advantage
Once your first customer experience AI implementation is successful, you can begin scaling across your entire customer journey. This is where small businesses can truly compete with enterprise-level customer experiences.

Multi-Touchpoint Integration Strategy:
- **Pre-purchase experience** - AI-powered lead qualification, product recommendations, and sales support
- **Purchase process** - Automated order processing, payment handling, and confirmation communications

- **Delivery and fulfillment** - Proactive shipping updates, delivery coordination, and issue resolution
- **Post-purchase support** - Automated follow-up, satisfaction surveys, and support ticket routing
- **Retention and expansion** - Personalized offers, renewal reminders, and upsell recommendations

Building Customer Experience Systems

The goal is creating interconnected AI systems that share customer data and insights across all touchpoints. This creates seamless experiences where customers never have to repeat information or explain their history.

Technology Stack Considerations:

- **Customer data platform** - Centralized storage for all customer information and interactions
- **Integration middleware** - Tools that connect different AI systems and business applications
- **Analytics dashboard** - Real-time monitoring of customer experience metrics across all touchpoints
- **Feedback collection systems** - Automated ways to gather customer input and satisfaction data

Your customer experience revolution starts with understanding that AI isn't about replacing human connection—it's about enhancing every opportunity to create meaningful relationships with your customers. The businesses that recognize this distinction will dominate their markets while competitors struggle to match their responsiveness, personalization, and overall customer satisfaction.

The next chapter will show you how to take everything you've learned about AI implementation and apply it to the back-office operations that run your business, creating systems that truly allow your business to operate itself while you focus on growth and strategy.

Chapter Fifteen

Operations That Run Themselves

Your business should work for you, not against you. The most successful small business owners aren't the ones who work the hardest—they're the ones who build systems that eliminate their daily involvement in routine operations. Once you implement AI-powered automation correctly, you'll discover what it feels like to have a business that truly serves your life goals rather than consuming every waking moment. This chapter reveals how to achieve operational freedom through strategic AI implementation.

The Hidden Cost of Manual Operations

Every morning, Sarah Chen opened her marketing agency knowing she'd spend the next ten hours juggling client schedules, managing inventory for promotional materials, and tracking project deadlines across multiple spreadsheets. Despite building a successful business with twelve employees, she felt trapped in a cycle of constant oversight and manual coordination.

Sarah's story isn't unique. Most small business owners become prisoners of their own success, trapped in operational details that prevent them from focusing on growth and strategy. They've built businesses that depend entirely on their daily involvement, creating what business experts call "owner dependency syndrome."

The real tragedy isn't the time lost—it's the opportunities missed. While you're managing schedules and tracking inventory, your competitors are developing new services, building strategic partnerships, and capturing market share. The solution isn't working harder or hiring more people. It's building intelligent systems that handle routine operations automatically.

The Mathematical Reality of Manual Operations

Consider the true cost of handling routine operations manually. The average small business owner spends 60% of their time on administrative tasks that could be automated. If you value your time at $100 per hour and work 50 hours weekly, that's $3,000 in lost strategic value every week—$156,000 annually.

But the hidden costs run deeper. Manual operations create bottlenecks that limit growth, increase error rates, and prevent you from scaling efficiently. Every process that requires your personal involvement becomes a constraint on your business's potential.

Shadow Implementation for Back-Office Automation

The SHADOW Framework transforms back-office operations by running AI systems parallel to your existing processes, proving their effectiveness before full implementation. This approach eliminates the fear of operational disruption while building confidence in automated solutions.

Screen Your Administrative Processes

Start by auditing your daily administrative tasks with brutal honesty. Track everything you do for one week, noting how much time each activity requires and how often it repeats. Most business owners discover they're spending 3-4 hours daily on tasks that AI can handle more efficiently.

Focus on processes that meet three criteria:

- **Repetitive**: Tasks you perform multiple times weekly
- **Rule-based**: Activities that follow consistent patterns
- **Time-consuming**: Processes requiring more than 30 minutes daily

Common high-impact opportunities include invoice processing, appointment scheduling, inventory tracking, expense categorization, and customer follow-up sequences. These processes typically offer 70-80% time savings when automated correctly.

Harvest Your Operational Data

AI systems require quality data to function effectively. Before implementing automation, you need clean, organized information about your current processes. This step often reveals inefficiencies you didn't know existed.

Document your current workflow patterns by collecting data on processing times, error rates, and resource requirements. For inventory management, gather historical ordering patterns, seasonal demand fluctuations, and supplier lead times. For scheduling, analyze appointment patterns, no-show rates, and resource utilization.

Create a baseline measurement system that tracks:
- Average processing time per task
- Monthly error rates and correction costs
- Staff hours dedicated to routine operations
- Customer satisfaction scores for administrative interactions

This documentation becomes your comparison benchmark for measuring AI performance improvements.

Acquire the Right Automation Tools

The automation software market can overwhelm small business owners with thousands of options. Focus on solutions that integrate easily with your existing systems and offer trial periods for risk-free testing.

Process Type	Recommended Solutions	Integration Complexity	Typical ROI Timeline
Invoice Processing	QuickBooks AI, Receipt Bank	Low	2-4 weeks
Appointment Scheduling	Calendly, Acuity	Low	1-2 weeks
Inventory Management	TradeGecko, Cin7	Medium	4-8 weeks
Customer Communication	HubSpot, Mailchimp	Medium	3-6 weeks
Expense Tracking	Expensify, Receipt Bank	Low	2-3 weeks

Choose solutions that offer API connectivity with your current software stack. Avoid platforms that require complete system overhauls—you want automation that enhances your existing operations, not replaces them entirely.

Deploy Your Parallel Operations System

Shadow implementation for back-office automation means running AI systems alongside your current processes for 30-60 days. This parallel approach lets you compare results directly while maintaining operational continuity.

Set up your AI system to process the same data your manual system handles, but don't rely on it for critical decisions yet. For example, let your AI invoice processing system categorize expenses while you continue your current approval process. Compare the AI's categorizations against your manual decisions to measure accuracy.

Monitor key performance indicators daily during the shadow period:
- **Processing speed**: How quickly does AI complete tasks versus manual methods?
- **Accuracy rates**: What percentage of AI decisions align with your manual choices?
- **Exception handling**: How well does the system manage unusual situations?
- **Integration stability**: Does the AI system disrupt existing workflows?

Optimize Performance Through Data Analysis

The shadow period generates valuable performance data that guides optimization efforts. Most AI systems require fine-tuning to match your specific business requirements and preferences.

Analyze patterns in AI decision-making to identify areas for improvement. If your expense categorization AI consistently misclassifies certain vendors, adjust the training parameters or create custom rules. If appointment scheduling AI books conflicting meetings, refine the availability algorithms.

Create feedback loops that improve system performance over time. Modern AI platforms learn from corrections, becoming more accurate as they process more of your data. Document these improvements to build confidence in the system's reliability.

Weave Automation Into Full Operations

Once your shadow testing proves AI effectiveness, transition to full operational integration. This process requires careful change management to ensure staff adoption and continued performance.

Develop transition protocols that phase out manual processes gradually. Start with low-risk operations like expense categorization, then progress to more critical functions like inventory ordering. This staged approach builds team confidence while minimizing disruption risks.

Train your team on monitoring and exception handling rather than replacing their roles entirely. AI systems work best when humans focus on strategic oversight and complex problem-solving rather than routine processing.

AI Solutions for Inventory, Scheduling, and Resource Optimization

Smart businesses use AI to anticipate needs rather than react to problems. The most powerful automation systems predict requirements and optimize resources before issues arise.

Predictive Inventory Management

Traditional inventory management reacts to stock levels—reordering when supplies run low. AI-powered systems analyze patterns to predict demand weeks or months in advance, optimizing ordering schedules and reducing carrying costs.

Implement demand forecasting AI that considers multiple variables:
- **Historical sales patterns** across different time periods
- **Seasonal trends** specific to your industry and location
- **Market conditions** that influence customer behavior
- **Promotional impacts** on product demand
- **Supplier lead times** and reliability patterns

Modern inventory AI can reduce carrying costs by 20-30% while decreasing stockout situations by 40-50%. The system learns your business patterns and adjusts predictions based on changing conditions.

Intelligent Resource Scheduling

Resource optimization AI transforms how you allocate staff time, equipment usage, and facility capacity. Instead of managing schedules reactively, you can optimize resource allocation based on predicted demand and efficiency patterns.

Deploy scheduling AI that considers:
- **Staff skill levels** and availability patterns
- **Equipment maintenance** requirements and capacity
- **Customer preferences** for timing and service providers
- **Travel time** and geographical constraints
- **Profit margins** for different service combinations

Advanced scheduling systems can increase resource utilization by 25-35% while improving customer satisfaction through better appointment availability and reduced wait times.

Automated Workflow Optimization

AI workflow systems analyze how tasks move through your organization, identifying bottlenecks and optimizing process sequences. These systems continuously adjust workflows based on current capacity and priority levels.

Implement workflow AI that monitors:

- **Task completion times** for different team members
- **Process dependencies** that create delays
- **Quality control** checkpoints and approval stages
- **Customer communication** touchpoints and response times
- **Resource allocation** efficiency across projects

Workflow optimization typically increases overall productivity by 30-40% while reducing project completion times and improving quality consistency.

Creating Systems That Free You From Daily Management

The ultimate goal of operational AI isn't efficiency—it's freedom. You want systems that make intelligent decisions without your constant oversight, allowing you to focus on vision, strategy, and growth.

Building Decision-Making Frameworks

AI systems need clear parameters for making autonomous decisions. Define decision trees that handle routine situations automatically while escalating complex issues for human review.

Create decision frameworks that specify:

- **Automatic approval** thresholds for different types of decisions
- **Escalation triggers** that require human intervention
- **Performance monitoring** that tracks decision quality
- **Learning mechanisms** that improve decision accuracy over time

Start with low-risk decisions like routine purchasing, appointment confirmations, and standard customer inquiries. Gradually expand AI decision-making authority as confidence builds.

Exception Management Protocols

No AI system handles every situation perfectly. Build robust exception management that identifies unusual circumstances and routes them appropriately. This approach maintains quality while preserving automation benefits.

Design exception protocols that:

- **Recognize unusual patterns** that fall outside normal parameters
- **Route complex issues** to appropriate team members
- **Track exception frequency** to identify system improvement opportunities
- **Document resolution patterns** to expand AI capability over time

Effective exception management ensures that automation enhances rather than constrains your business flexibility.

Performance Monitoring Dashboards

Create monitoring systems that provide real-time visibility into AI performance without requiring constant attention. These dashboards should alert you to significant issues while providing confidence that systems are functioning correctly.

Build dashboards that track:

- **Key performance indicators** for each automated process
- **Cost savings** generated through automation
- **Error rates** and quality metrics
- **Customer satisfaction** impacts from automated interactions
- **Staff productivity** improvements from reduced manual work

Modern dashboard tools can send automated alerts when performance drops below acceptable thresholds, ensuring you stay informed without constant monitoring.

Continuous Improvement Mechanisms

The best operational AI systems improve automatically over time. Build feedback loops that enhance performance based on results and changing business conditions.

Implement improvement systems that:

- **Analyze performance trends** to identify optimization opportunities
- **Incorporate new data** to improve prediction accuracy
- **Adjust parameters** based on changing business conditions

- **Update decision rules** as policies and preferences evolve
- **Expand capabilities** as confidence and expertise grow

This continuous improvement approach ensures your automation systems evolve with your business rather than becoming outdated constraints.

The Financial Impact of Self-Running Operations

Operational automation delivers measurable financial benefits that compound over time. Understanding these benefits helps justify investment and guides implementation priorities.

Direct Cost Savings

Automation reduces labor costs for routine operations while improving consistency and speed. Most small businesses achieve 40-60% cost reductions in automated processes within six months of implementation.

Calculate direct savings by comparing:
- **Staff hours** saved through automation
- **Error reduction** costs from improved accuracy
- **Overtime elimination** from efficient resource scheduling
- **Vendor cost optimization** through better purchasing decisions

Indirect Revenue Benefits

Self-running operations free your time for revenue-generating activities. This indirect benefit often exceeds direct cost savings as you focus on business development, strategic partnerships, and innovation.

Track indirect benefits including:
- **New business development** time created through automation
- **Customer satisfaction** improvements from consistent service
- **Strategic planning** capacity for long-term growth
- **Innovation opportunities** explored with freed-up resources

Scalability Advantages

Automated operations scale efficiently without proportional increases in management overhead. This scalability advantage becomes increasingly valuable as your business grows.

Document scalability benefits such as:
- **Revenue growth** without equivalent staff increases
- **Market expansion** capability through operational efficiency
- **Service quality** consistency across larger customer bases
- **Competitive positioning** through superior operational performance

Overcoming Implementation Challenges

Even with careful planning, operational automation presents challenges that require strategic solutions. Understanding common obstacles and their solutions prevents implementation delays and builds confidence.

Staff Resistance to Change

Team members often fear that automation threatens their job security. Address these concerns through transparent communication and role redefinition rather than replacement.

Manage change resistance by:
- **Explaining automation benefits** for both business and individual development
- **Redefining roles** toward higher-value activities rather than routine processing
- **Providing training** for new skills and responsibilities
- **Celebrating successes** that demonstrate positive impacts
- **Involving staff** in automation planning and optimization

Integration Complexity

Connecting AI systems with existing software can create technical challenges. Minimize complexity by choosing solutions with proven integration capabilities and professional support.

Simplify integration through:
- **API-first solutions** that connect easily with existing systems
- **Professional implementation** support from vendors
- **Phased rollouts** that test integration before full deployment
- **Backup procedures** that maintain operations during transitions
- **Performance monitoring** that identifies integration issues quickly

Quality Control Concerns

Business owners worry that automation might reduce quality or create customer service problems. Address these concerns through careful monitoring and gradual implementation.

Maintain quality through:
- **Shadow testing** that proves performance before full implementation
- **Quality metrics** that track customer satisfaction and operational performance
- **Exception handling** that routes complex issues to human oversight
- **Continuous monitoring** that identifies and corrects problems quickly
- **Customer feedback** systems that capture satisfaction and improvement opportunities

Building Long-Term Operational Excellence

Self-running operations represent the foundation for sustainable business growth. Once you achieve operational freedom, you can focus on strategic initiatives that create lasting competitive advantages.

Strategic Planning Capacity

Freed from daily operational management, you can invest time in strategic planning, market analysis, and innovation. This strategic focus often generates more value than the operational savings themselves.

Use newfound time for:
- **Market opportunity** analysis and business development
- **Competitive intelligence** gathering and strategic response
- **Innovation projects** that differentiate your offerings
- **Partnership development** that expands market reach
- **Team development** that builds organizational capability

Competitive Positioning

Businesses with self-running operations can respond more quickly to market changes and customer demands. This agility becomes a significant competitive advantage in rapidly changing markets.

Leverage operational excellence for:
- **Faster service delivery** that exceeds customer expectations
- **Cost advantages** that support competitive pricing
- **Quality consistency** that builds brand reputation

- **Innovation capacity** that creates market differentiation
- **Growth scalability** that captures market opportunities

Personal Freedom and Satisfaction

The ultimate benefit of self-running operations is personal freedom—the ability to build a business that serves your life goals rather than consuming all your time and energy.

Operational freedom enables:
- **Work-life balance** that supports personal relationships and interests
- **Travel flexibility** without operational disruption
- **Stress reduction** from automated systems handling routine problems
- **Growth enjoyment** rather than growth anxiety from operational complexity
- **Legacy building** through systems that outlast individual involvement

As you progress through implementing self-running operations, you'll discover that the real value isn't just efficiency—it's the transformation from business owner to business architect. You'll design systems that work without you, creating freedom to focus on what truly matters: vision, strategy, and the meaningful impact your business creates in the world.

The next chapter explores how to revolutionize your customer experience through AI implementation, building on the operational foundation you've created to deliver service levels that distinguish your business from competitors and create lasting customer loyalty.

Chapter Sixteen

Marketing Like a Fortune 500 Company

Small businesses can now access Fortune 500 marketing power through AI. The marketing playing field has leveled in ways that would have seemed impossible just five years ago. What once required massive budgets, dedicated data science teams, and enterprise-grade software suites is now available to any business owner willing to embrace intelligent automation. Your local competitor who's still running Facebook ads the same way they did in 2019 won't know what hit them.

The Great Marketing Equalizer Has Arrived

The old rules of marketing don't apply anymore. Where large corporations once dominated through sheer spending power and sophisticated analytics teams, AI has democratized access to world-class marketing intelligence. Today's small business owner can deploy the same predictive analytics, customer segmentation, and campaign optimization tools that Fortune 500 companies use—often at a fraction of the cost and with faster implementation times.

Consider how Netflix recommends content to millions of users or how Amazon personalizes product suggestions for each visitor. These same AI-driven personalization engines are now accessible to businesses with 10 employees and modest marketing budgets. The technology that powers billion-dollar marketing operations can be yours within weeks, not years.

But here's where most small business owners get stuck: they see the potential but don't know how to implement these tools without risking their current marketing efforts.

They're caught between the fear of falling behind and the terror of disrupting what's already working. This is exactly where the Shadow Implementation Method becomes your competitive advantage.

Why Traditional Marketing Approaches Fall Short

Traditional marketing for small businesses follows a predictable pattern: create content, post on social media, run some ads, hope for the best, and measure results weeks later. This approach worked when everyone played by the same rules, but AI has changed the game entirely.

Your competitors who embrace AI marketing can now:

- **Predict customer behavior** before customers know what they want
- **Personalize content** for each individual visitor in real-time
- **Optimize campaigns** automatically while you're sleeping
- **Identify high-value prospects** before they even visit your website
- **Create content** that resonates with specific customer segments

Meanwhile, businesses stuck in traditional marketing modes are essentially bringing calculators to a supercomputer fight. They're working harder, spending more, and getting fewer results because they're competing with outdated tools.

The shift isn't subtle—it's seismic. AI-powered marketing tools can analyze customer data, predict purchasing patterns, and optimize campaigns at speeds and scales impossible for human marketers. While you're manually adjusting ad spending based on last week's performance, AI-driven competitors are making real-time optimizations based on hundreds of data points you can't even see.

Applying SHADOW to Marketing AI Implementation

The beauty of implementing marketing AI through the Shadow Framework lies in its risk-free testing approach. You don't need to abandon your current marketing efforts or bet your entire budget on unproven tools. Instead, you'll run AI marketing solutions parallel to your existing campaigns, allowing you to validate their effectiveness before making any commitments.

Here's how the SHADOW Framework applies specifically to marketing AI implementation:

Screen Your Marketing Opportunities

Start by auditing your current marketing processes to identify the highest-impact areas for AI implementation. Look for repetitive tasks that consume significant time, campaigns that require constant manual optimization, or customer data that you're not fully utilizing.

The most profitable AI marketing opportunities typically fall into these categories:

1. Customer segmentation and targeting - Moving from broad demographics to behavioral prediction

2. Content personalization - Delivering the right message to the right person at the right time

3. Campaign optimization - Automated bid management and budget allocation

4. Lead scoring and qualification - Identifying which prospects are most likely to convert

5. Email marketing automation - Triggered sequences based on customer behavior

6. Social media management - Automated posting and engagement optimization

Calculate the potential time savings and revenue increases for each opportunity. Focus on the area where you currently spend the most time on manual tasks or where small improvements could yield significant results.

Harvest Your Marketing Data and Resources

Before implementing any AI marketing solution, you need to gather the essential ingredients for success. This includes:

Historical Performance Data: Collect at least 90 days of campaign performance metrics from all your current marketing channels. AI tools need this baseline data to understand your customer patterns and optimize accordingly.

Customer Information: Compile existing customer data including purchase history, website behavior, email engagement, and demographic information. The richer your customer data, the more effectively AI can segment and target your audience.

Content Assets: Organize your existing marketing content including blog posts, videos, images, and ad copy. AI tools can analyze this content to understand what resonates with your audience and suggest optimizations.

Budget Allocation: Determine how much you're willing to invest in testing AI marketing tools. Start with 10-20% of your current marketing budget for parallel testing—enough to generate meaningful data without risking your core marketing efforts.

Team Buy-in: Identify one team member who will champion the AI implementation and monitor results. This person doesn't need technical expertise but should be comfortable with data analysis and willing to learn new tools.

Acquire the Right AI Marketing Solution

The marketing AI tool market can feel overwhelming, with hundreds of options claiming to revolutionize your marketing efforts. Cut through the noise by focusing on solutions that integrate easily with your existing tools and require minimal technical setup.

Evaluation Framework for Marketing AI Tools:

Criteria	Weight	What to Look For
Ease of Integration	30%	Direct connections to your current CRM, email platform, and advertising accounts
Trial Period Availability	25%	At least 30-day free trial or money-back guarantee
Learning Curve	20%	User-friendly interface that doesn't require technical training
Support Quality	15%	Responsive customer support with implementation assistance
Pricing Transparency	10%	Clear pricing structure without hidden fees or setup costs

Top Categories of Marketing AI Tools for Small Businesses:

1. All-in-One Marketing Platforms - Tools like HubSpot or Mailchimp that integrate multiple AI features

2. Social Media AI - Platforms like Hootsuite Insights or Sprout Social for automated posting and engagement

3. Email Marketing AI - Services like ConvertKit or ActiveCampaign with behavioral triggers

4. Advertising AI - Tools like Google's Smart Campaigns or Facebook's Automatic Placements

5. Analytics and Insights - Platforms like Google Analytics Intelligence or customer data platforms

Start with one tool in your highest-priority area rather than trying to implement multiple solutions simultaneously. Once you've proven success with your first AI marketing tool, you can expand to other areas.

Deploy Your Parallel Marketing System

The deployment phase is where the Shadow Method truly shines in marketing applications. Instead of replacing your current marketing efforts, you'll run AI-powered campaigns alongside your existing approach, allowing for direct performance comparisons.

Parallel Deployment Strategy:

Weeks 1-2: Baseline Establishment

- Continue running your current marketing campaigns exactly as before
- Set up tracking systems to monitor all current campaign metrics
- Install your chosen AI marketing tool and complete initial configuration
- Import historical data and connect integrations

Weeks 3-4: Shadow Launch

- Launch AI-powered campaigns targeting the same audience segments as your traditional campaigns
- Maintain identical budgets between traditional and AI campaigns for fair comparison
- Monitor both systems daily but make no optimizations to either approach
- Document any technical issues or learning curve challenges

Weeks 5-6: Performance Monitoring

- Analyze performance differences between traditional and AI campaigns
- Track key metrics including cost per acquisition, conversion rates, and return on ad spend
- Identify specific areas where AI shows improvement or underperformance
- Gather feedback from team members using the new tools

The parallel approach eliminates the risk of campaign failure while providing concrete data about AI effectiveness. You're not betting your marketing success on untested tools—you're conducting a controlled experiment with minimal downside risk.

Advanced AI Marketing Strategies That Level the Playing Field

Once you've successfully implemented your first AI marketing tool through the Shadow Method, you're ready to explore advanced strategies that give small businesses Fortune 500-level capabilities.

Predictive Customer Analytics

The most powerful advantage of AI marketing isn't just automating what you already do—it's gaining insights that human analysis can't uncover. Predictive analytics allows you to identify which customers are most likely to make repeat purchases, which prospects are ready to buy, and which segments offer the highest lifetime value.

Implementation Strategy:

- Use AI tools to analyze customer purchase patterns and identify early indicators of high-value customers
- Create predictive models that score leads based on their likelihood to convert
- Develop retention campaigns targeting customers most at risk of churning
- Optimize inventory and product recommendations based on demand forecasting

Real-Time Personalization

While large corporations have teams of data scientists creating personalization algorithms, AI tools now make sophisticated personalization accessible to any business. Your website can dynamically adjust content, product recommendations, and messaging based on each visitor's behavior and characteristics.

Key Personalization Opportunities:

- **Website Content:** Display different headlines, images, and calls-to-action based on visitor source and behavior
- **Email Campaigns:** Customize subject lines, content, and send times for each subscriber
- **Product Recommendations:** Show relevant products based on browsing history and similar customer purchases
- **Ad Targeting:** Create lookalike audiences based on your best customers and optimize targeting automatically

Cross-Channel Campaign Orchestration

The most sophisticated marketing AI tools can coordinate campaigns across multiple channels, ensuring consistent messaging while optimizing each channel for its unique strengths. This level of coordination was previously only available to enterprises with dedicated marketing operations teams.

Orchestration Benefits:

- Consistent brand messaging across email, social media, and advertising
- Coordinated timing to avoid message fatigue and maximize impact

- Cross-channel data sharing for better audience insights
- Unified attribution tracking to understand the customer journey

Optimize Performance and Prove ROI

The optimization phase is where AI marketing truly demonstrates its superiority over traditional approaches. While human marketers can analyze campaign performance weekly or monthly, AI systems optimize continuously, making thousands of micro-adjustments that compound into significant improvements.

Key Optimization Areas:

Budget Allocation Intelligence

AI marketing tools excel at dynamic budget allocation, automatically shifting spending toward the highest-performing campaigns, audiences, and channels. Instead of manually checking campaign performance and making adjustments, AI monitors performance in real-time and optimizes spending to maximize return on investment.

Audience Refinement

Traditional marketing relies on broad demographic targeting, but AI can identify behavioral patterns and micro-segments that human analysis misses. Your AI tools will continuously refine audience targeting based on conversion data, identifying the specific characteristics that predict customer behavior.

Creative Optimization

AI can test dozens of ad variations simultaneously, identifying which images, headlines, and calls-to-action perform best for specific audience segments. This level of creative testing and optimization would be impossible to manage manually but happens automatically with AI tools.

Timing Optimization

AI marketing platforms analyze when your specific audience is most likely to engage with content, make purchases, or respond to ads. Instead of guessing optimal posting times or email send schedules, AI identifies the precise moments when your audience is most receptive.

ROI Documentation Framework:

Create a comprehensive performance tracking system that demonstrates the value of your AI marketing investments:

Metric Category	Traditional Marketing	AI-Enhanced Marketing	Improvement
Cost Per Acquisition	Track manually weekly	Tracked automatically daily	% improvement
Conversion Rate	Campaign-level analysis	Segment-specific optimization	% improvement
Customer Lifetime Value	Historical averages	Predictive modeling	% improvement
Time Savings	Hours spent on optimization	Automated optimization	Hours saved
Revenue Attribution	Last-click attribution	Multi-touch attribution	% accuracy gain

This documentation serves multiple purposes: it justifies your AI marketing investments, provides data for scaling decisions, and creates compelling case studies for future implementations.

Weave AI Marketing Into Full Operations

The final phase of Shadow Implementation involves integrating your proven AI marketing tools into your complete business operations. This isn't just about making AI marketing your primary approach—it's about connecting marketing AI with your sales, customer service, and product development processes.

Integration Points for Maximum Impact:

Sales and Marketing Alignment

Connect your AI marketing insights with your sales process to create a seamless customer experience. Marketing AI can identify when prospects are ready to buy and automatically trigger sales outreach, while sales feedback can improve marketing targeting and messaging.

Customer Service Enhancement

Use marketing AI data to personalize customer service interactions. When customers contact support, representatives can see their complete interaction history, preferences, and predicted needs, enabling more effective and personalized service.

Product Development Insights

Marketing AI generates valuable data about customer preferences, behavior patterns, and unmet needs. This information can guide product development decisions, helping you create offerings that align with actual customer demand rather than assumptions.

Financial Planning Integration

AI marketing tools provide more accurate revenue forecasting and customer acquisition cost predictions, enabling better financial planning and resource allocation decisions.

The Competitive Advantage Timeline

Understanding the timeline of competitive advantage helps you appreciate why starting before you're ready matters so much in AI marketing implementation.

Months 1-2: Foundation Phase

While you're implementing your first AI marketing tools through Shadow Method, you're building capabilities that competitors don't have. You're learning how AI tools work, gathering performance data, and developing expertise that will compound over time.

Months 3-6: Acceleration Phase

Your AI marketing tools are now optimized and integrated into your operations. You're achieving better results than traditional marketing approaches while spending less time on manual optimization. Competitors who haven't started AI implementation are falling further behind.

Months 6-12: Dominance Phase

You've expanded AI across multiple marketing channels and developed sophisticated automation that runs efficiently with minimal oversight. Your customer acquisition costs are lower, conversion rates are higher, and you have predictive insights that guide strategic decisions. Traditional competitors can't match your efficiency or effectiveness.

Year 2 and Beyond: Market Leadership

Your AI marketing capabilities are so advanced that new competitors can't catch up quickly. You have years of optimization data, refined processes, and integrated systems that create sustainable competitive advantages. You're not just using AI marketing—you're leading your industry in marketing innovation.

The companies that start AI marketing implementation today will have insurmountable advantages over those who wait for perfect readiness. Every month of delay means falling further behind competitors who are already building these capabilities.

Common Implementation Challenges and Solutions

Even with the Shadow Method's risk-mitigation approach, you'll encounter challenges during AI marketing implementation. Anticipating these obstacles and having solutions ready ensures smooth execution.

Challenge 1: Data Quality Issues

Many small businesses discover their customer data is incomplete or inconsistent when they start implementing AI marketing tools. Missing email addresses, duplicate records, and outdated information can limit AI effectiveness.

Solution: Start a data cleanup process parallel to your AI implementation. Use this opportunity to improve your overall customer data management practices, not just for AI but for all business operations.

Challenge 2: Learning Curve Resistance

Team members may resist learning new AI marketing tools, especially if they're comfortable with current processes or worried about job security.

Solution: Frame AI implementation as augmentation, not replacement. Show team members how AI tools eliminate tedious tasks and enable them to focus on strategic, creative work that's more engaging and valuable.

Challenge 3: Integration Complexity

Connecting AI marketing tools with existing systems can be more complex than anticipated, especially with older CRM or email marketing platforms.

Solution: Choose AI tools with robust integration capabilities and consider this a catalyst for upgrading outdated marketing infrastructure. The long-term benefits of modern, integrated systems far outweigh short-term implementation challenges.

Challenge 4: Unrealistic Expectations

Some business owners expect immediate, dramatic results from AI marketing implementation and become disappointed when improvements are gradual.

Solution: Set realistic expectations about AI optimization timelines. Emphasize that AI marketing success comes from continuous improvement over time, not overnight transformation.

Your journey into AI-powered marketing represents more than just adopting new tools—it's about fundamentally changing how your business competes in the modern marketplace. The strategies and frameworks you've learned in this chapter give you the same capabilities as Fortune 500 marketing departments, but with the agility and speed that only small businesses possess.

As you move forward with AI marketing implementation, you'll discover that the technology itself is just the beginning. The real transformation happens when AI marketing connects with every aspect of your business operations, creating integrated systems that drive growth automatically. Our next chapter explores how to achieve this ultimate goal: building operations that run themselves through strategic AI automation.

Chapter Seventeen

Financial Intelligence and Forecasting

AI TRANSFORMS YOUR FINANCIAL guesswork into business superpowers. Gone are the days when you'd stare at spreadsheets wondering if you could afford that new hire or whether seasonal dips would crush your cash flow. AI doesn't just crunch numbers—it reveals patterns, predicts challenges, and gives you the financial foresight that Fortune 500 companies have enjoyed for decades. Now you can make decisions with the confidence that comes from knowing exactly what your numbers mean and where they're heading.

The financial stress that keeps you awake at 3 AM? AI eliminates it by replacing uncertainty with data-driven clarity that lets you sleep soundly knowing your business is on solid ground.

The Crystal Ball Every Business Owner Dreams About

You've probably wished for a crystal ball that could tell you exactly when to expand, when to tighten your belt, and when golden opportunities will knock on your door. That crystal ball exists—it's called AI-powered financial intelligence, and it's no longer reserved for massive corporations with billion-dollar budgets.

Traditional financial management feels like driving at night with broken headlights. You can see just enough to avoid immediate crashes, but you're constantly worried about what's coming around the next curve. AI flips on the high beams and gives you night vision goggles, illuminating the road miles ahead.

Here's what changes when you implement AI financial intelligence:
- **Predictive accuracy** that spots cash flow problems 3-6 months before they hit
- **Pattern recognition** that identifies your most profitable customers and products
- **Scenario modeling** that shows you exactly how decisions will impact your bottom line
- **Risk assessment** that flags potential problems before they become expensive mistakes
- **Optimization recommendations** that find money you didn't know you were leaving on the table

The best part? You don't need a finance degree or expensive consultants to access these capabilities. AI democratizes financial intelligence, making sophisticated analysis as simple as asking the right questions.

Breaking Free from Spreadsheet Prison

Let's be honest—your current financial system probably involves too many spreadsheets, too much guesswork, and too many sleepless nights wondering if you're making the right choices. You're not alone. Most small business owners operate in what I call "spreadsheet prison"—trapped in manual processes that eat time without providing real insights.

Traditional financial reporting tells you what happened last month. AI financial intelligence tells you what's going to happen next quarter and gives you the tools to influence those outcomes. That's the difference between reactive management and strategic leadership.

Consider this scenario: Your traditional approach might show you that sales dipped 15% in March. AI financial intelligence would have predicted that dip in January, identified the contributing factors, and recommended specific actions to minimize the impact. By the time March arrived, you'd already be executing countermeasures instead of scrambling to understand what went wrong.

The Shadow Implementation Advantage for Financial AI

Remember our Shadow Implementation Method? It's perfect for financial AI because you can run predictive models alongside your existing accounting systems without disrupting day-to-day operations. You'll validate AI insights against real outcomes while building confidence in the technology's accuracy.

Here's how shadow implementation works for financial intelligence:
1. **Parallel tracking** - Run AI analysis alongside your current financial reports

2. **Performance comparison** - Measure AI predictions against actual results
3. **Gradual integration** - Slowly incorporate AI insights into decision-making
4. **Risk mitigation** - Maintain existing processes while proving AI value
5. **Confidence building** - Develop trust in AI recommendations through verified accuracy

AI Applications That Transform Financial Decision-Making

Modern AI financial tools tackle the specific challenges that keep small business owners up at night. Let's explore the applications that deliver immediate value without requiring technical expertise.

Cash Flow Forecasting That Actually Works

Traditional cash flow forecasting often feels like educated guessing. You look at historical patterns, factor in known variables, and hope for the best. AI cash flow forecasting analyzes hundreds of variables you'd never think to consider:

- **Seasonal patterns** in your industry and local market
- **Customer payment behaviors** based on invoice amounts and timing
- **Economic indicators** that affect your business sector
- **Weather patterns** that influence customer behavior
- **Market trends** that impact demand for your products or services

Traditional Method	AI-Enhanced Method
Monthly projections	Daily cash flow predictions
60% accuracy rate	85-95% accuracy rate
Based on 3-5 variables	Analyzes 50+ variables
Manual updates required	Automatic real-time updates
Generic industry assumptions	Business-specific patterns

The result? You'll know exactly when cash will be tight and can take preventive action weeks or months in advance. No more emergency loans or missed opportunities because you didn't have the financial foresight to prepare.

Expense Optimization Through Pattern Recognition

AI excels at finding patterns humans miss, especially in expense management. Your AI financial intelligence system will identify spending patterns that are costing you money without providing proportional value.

For example, AI might discover that:
- Your software subscriptions cost 40% more than necessary due to overlapping features
- Certain vendors consistently deliver late, costing you opportunity costs
- Your inventory levels are optimized for last year's demand patterns, not current trends
- Marketing spend in specific channels generates diminishing returns after certain thresholds

These insights come from analyzing your financial data against industry benchmarks, seasonal patterns, and performance correlations that would take human analysts weeks to identify.

Revenue Forecasting with Precision

AI revenue forecasting goes far beyond simple trend analysis. It considers:

Customer Behavior Patterns
- Purchase frequency changes that signal opportunity or risk
- Customer lifetime value predictions based on engagement metrics
- Churn probability calculations that identify at-risk revenue
- Upselling opportunities based on purchase history analysis

Market Dynamics
- Competitive pricing impacts on your revenue potential
- Economic indicators that influence customer spending
- Seasonal variations specific to your business model
- Industry trends that affect demand for your offerings

Product Performance Intelligence
- Which products drive the highest margins
- Cross-selling opportunities you're currently missing
- Inventory optimization to maximize revenue per square foot
- Pricing elasticity analysis to optimize profit margins

Risk Management Through AI-Powered Business Intelligence

Financial risk management traditionally relies on hindsight and general industry wisdom. AI risk management provides foresight and business-specific intelligence that protects your company from potential threats while identifying opportunities others miss.

Early Warning Systems That Actually Warn Early

AI creates sophisticated early warning systems that monitor hundreds of risk indicators simultaneously. These systems alert you to potential problems while you still have time to address them effectively.

Customer Risk Indicators

- Payment pattern changes that signal financial distress
- Order frequency shifts that predict customer churn
- Communication pattern changes that indicate dissatisfaction
- Credit score fluctuations that affect payment reliability

Operational Risk Signals

- Supplier performance degradation before it impacts your operations
- Employee productivity patterns that predict turnover
- System performance metrics that forecast equipment failures
- Compliance requirements that could affect your operations

Market Risk Analysis

- Competitive threats emerging in your space
- Economic indicators that could impact your industry
- Regulatory changes that might affect your business model
- Technology shifts that could disrupt your operations

Scenario Planning That Prepares You for Anything

AI scenario planning goes beyond simple "what if" analysis. It creates comprehensive models that show you exactly how different situations would impact your business and what actions would optimize outcomes.

Economic Scenario Modeling

- Recession impact analysis with specific recommendations
- Interest rate change effects on your financing costs

- Inflation impact on your cost structure and pricing strategy
- Economic growth scenarios and how to capitalize on them

Competitive Scenario Analysis

- New competitor entry impact on your market share
- Pricing war scenarios and optimal response strategies
- Partnership opportunity evaluation
- Market expansion timing and resource requirements

Operational Scenario Planning

- Key employee departure impact and mitigation strategies
- Supplier disruption scenarios and alternative sourcing plans
- Technology failure recovery plans and backup systems
- Expansion scenario modeling with resource requirements

Cash Flow Optimization and Predictive Financial Modeling

Cash flow optimization through AI goes far beyond traditional accounts receivable management. It creates a complete financial ecosystem that maximizes liquidity while minimizing opportunity costs.

Working Capital Optimization

AI analyzes your entire cash conversion cycle to identify optimization opportunities:

Accounts Receivable Enhancement

- Customer payment pattern analysis to optimize collection timing
- Credit risk assessment to minimize bad debt exposure
- Payment method optimization to reduce processing costs
- Invoice timing optimization to improve cash flow

Inventory Intelligence

- Demand forecasting to minimize carrying costs
- Supplier payment timing optimization
- Seasonal inventory planning based on predictive models
- Product mix optimization for maximum profitability

Accounts Payable Strategy

- Vendor payment timing optimization to maximize cash availability

- Early payment discount analysis for cost-benefit optimization
- Supplier negotiation insights based on payment pattern analysis
- Cash flow timing coordination across all payment obligations

Predictive Financial Modeling for Strategic Planning

AI predictive modeling transforms strategic planning from guesswork into scientific analysis. You'll make expansion decisions, hiring choices, and investment commitments based on data-driven projections rather than gut feelings.

Growth Scenario Modeling

Your AI system will model various growth scenarios with specific financial requirements:

1. Conservative Growth (10-15% annual increase)
- Resource requirements and timin
- Cash flow implications and financing need
- Risk factors and mitigation strategie
- Profitability timeline and milestones

2. Aggressive Growth (25-40% annual increase
- Capital requirements and sourcing options
- Operational scaling challenges and solutions
- Market capture strategies and competitive responses
- Break-even analysis and return on investment

3. Acquisition Growth (growth through strategic purchases)
- Target identification and valuation criteria
- Integration cost analysis and timeline
- Synergy identification and realization plans
- Financing structure optimization

Investment Decision Intelligence

AI helps you evaluate investment opportunities with sophisticated analysis:
- **Equipment purchases:** ROI calculation including opportunity costs
- **Technology investments:** Productivity gains and competitive advantages
- **Marketing campaigns:** Expected return and optimization strategies
- **Staff additions:** Revenue per employee analysis and growth projections

Implementation Strategy Using the Shadow Method

Implementing AI financial intelligence using our Shadow Implementation Method ensures you gain confidence in the technology while maintaining your existing financial processes.

Phase 1: Screen Your Financial Opportunities

Start by identifying the financial challenge that causes you the most stress or costs the most money. Common high-impact opportunities include:

- **Cash flow prediction** if you frequently face liquidity challenges
- **Expense optimization** if costs seem to creep up without clear explanations
- **Revenue forecasting** if you struggle with demand planning and inventory management
- **Risk assessment** if you've experienced unexpected financial setbacks

Phase 2: Harvest Your Financial Data

Gather the historical data needed to train your AI system:

- Three years of financial statements (minimum)
- Customer payment history and patterns
- Vendor payment records and terms
- Inventory turnover data
- Seasonal sales patterns
- Marketing spend and revenue correlations

Phase 3: Acquire Your AI Financial Solution

Select a financial AI platform that integrates with your existing accounting system. Look for solutions that offer:

- **Easy integration** with QuickBooks, Xero, or your current accounting software
- **User-friendly dashboards** that present insights in plain English
- **Customizable alerts** for the metrics that matter most to your business
- **Mobile access** so you can monitor key indicators anywhere
- **Trial periods** that let you validate effectiveness before full commitment

Phase 4: Deploy Your Parallel Financial Intelligence

Run your AI financial system alongside existing processes for 60 days:

- Compare AI predictions with actual results
- Validate expense optimization recommendations

- Test cash flow forecasting accuracy
- Evaluate risk assessment reliability

Phase 5: Optimize Performance and Prove Value

Fine-tune your AI system based on real-world performance:

- Adjust prediction parameters for maximum accuracy
- Customize alerts for optimal timing and relevance
- Refine optimization recommendations based on implementation results
- Document financial improvements and cost savings

Phase 6: Weave AI Intelligence Into Daily Operations

Integrate proven AI insights into your regular decision-making process:

- Replace manual forecasting with AI predictions
- Implement automated alerts for critical financial metrics
- Use AI recommendations for major financial decisions
- Train staff on interpreting and acting on AI insights

Measuring Success and ROI

Track specific metrics to prove your AI financial intelligence investment delivers measurable value:

Accuracy Improvements

- Cash flow forecasting accuracy improvement (target: 20-30% better than manual methods)
- Expense variance reduction (target: 15-25% closer to budget)
- Revenue prediction accuracy (target: 85%+ accuracy rate)

Time Savings

- Reduction in time spent on financial analysis (target: 50-70% time savings)
- Faster decision-making cycles (target: 2-3x faster than previous methods)
- Automated report generation (target: 80% reduction in manual reporting time)

Financial Impact

- Cost reduction through expense optimization (target: 5-15% expense reduction)
- Improved cash flow management (target: 20-30% reduction in cash flow emergencies)
- Better investment decisions (target: 15-25% improvement in ROI on major purchases)

Common Pitfalls and How to Avoid Them

Data Quality Issues

Poor data quality will undermine AI accuracy. Ensure your financial data is clean, complete, and consistently formatted before implementing AI solutions.

Over-Reliance on Automation

AI should enhance human judgment, not replace it. Use AI insights to inform decisions while maintaining oversight and common-sense checks.

Inadequate Staff Training

Your team needs to understand how to interpret and act on AI insights. Invest in training to ensure effective adoption and utilization.

Unrealistic Expectations

AI improves financial intelligence significantly but isn't magic. Set realistic expectations for accuracy improvements and implementation timelines.

The Competitive Advantage of Financial Intelligence

When you implement AI financial intelligence successfully, you gain competitive advantages that compound over time:

Faster Decision Making

While competitors debate and analyze, you make informed decisions quickly based on AI insights and projections.

Better Resource Allocation

You invest time and money in opportunities with the highest returns while avoiding costly mistakes that drain resources.

Improved Negotiation Position

Armed with detailed financial intelligence, you negotiate better deals with vendors, customers, and partners.

Enhanced Credibility

Bankers, investors, and partners respect businesses that demonstrate sophisticated financial management and planning capabilities.

Financial intelligence through AI transforms you from someone who reacts to financial challenges into someone who anticipates and prevents them. You'll make decisions with confidence, sleep better at night, and build a business that's financially resilient and strategically positioned for growth.

The crystal ball insights you've always wanted are within reach—the only question is how quickly you'll embrace them and leave your financially stressed competitors behind.

Having established your financial intelligence foundation, you're ready to discover how these same AI principles can elevate your status from follower to leader. In our next chapter, we'll explore how to position yourself as the AI innovator in your industry, creating new opportunities and revenue streams while establishing the thought leadership that attracts customers, partners, and recognition.

Chapter Eighteen

Becoming the AI Leader in Your Industry

Your AI success story becomes your most powerful business card. When you've successfully implemented AI solutions that drive real results, you're no longer just another small business owner hoping to compete—you're the innovative leader others want to learn from, partner with, and hire. This shift from follower to leader opens doors you never imagined possible and creates revenue streams that compound your original AI investment. The transformation from AI implementer to industry thought leader isn't just about recognition; it's about building sustainable competitive advantages that extend far beyond operational efficiency.

Most business owners make the mistake of keeping their AI wins to themselves, thinking that secrecy protects their competitive edge. But here's what the smartest entrepreneurs understand: sharing your expertise strategically actually strengthens your market position while creating multiple new revenue opportunities. When you become known as the business owner who "figured out AI first," you attract high-value clients, partnership opportunities, and industry recognition that money can't buy. Your proven track record becomes a magnet for the exact opportunities that accelerate business growth.

The Authority Advantage

When you've successfully implemented AI in your business, you possess something incredibly valuable: proven expertise backed by real results. This isn't theoretical knowledge or academic understanding—it's battle-tested experience that other business owners desperately need. The gap between those who've successfully implemented AI and those still struggling with basic adoption creates an enormous opportunity for positioning yourself as the go-to expert in your industry.

Authority in the AI space isn't about having the most technical knowledge or the biggest budget. It's about having walked the path, overcome the challenges, and achieved measurable results that others can see and verify. Your journey from AI-paralyzed to AI-powered gives you credibility that consultants and academics simply can't match. You've faced the real-world implementation challenges, solved the practical problems, and can speak authentically about what actually works.

The key components of AI authority include:

1. **Documented Results** - Specific metrics and improvements you can share
2. **Implementation Stories** - Real challenges faced and how you overcame them
3. **Practical Insights** - Lessons learned that save others time and money
4. **Ongoing Innovation** - Continuous improvement and expansion of AI capabilities

This authority becomes the foundation for everything else you'll build as an industry leader. It's what gives weight to your words, credibility to your advice, and value to your services.

Strategic Positioning for Maximum Impact

Becoming an AI leader isn't about being the loudest voice in the room—it's about being the most trusted one. Strategic positioning means carefully crafting how you present your AI expertise to maximize impact while building authentic relationships within your industry. The goal is to become the person others think of first when AI topics arise in conversations, planning sessions, or strategic discussions.

Your positioning strategy should focus on three core elements: **accessibility, authenticity, and actionability**. You want to be seen as approachable rather than intimidating, genuine rather than boastful, and practical rather than theoretical. This means sharing your failures along with your successes, admitting what you don't know, and always focusing on how your experience can help others achieve similar results.

***Effective positioning strategies include*:**

- **Industry-Specific Focus**: Tailor your message to the unique challenges and opportunities within your specific industry
- **Results-Based Messaging**: Lead with concrete outcomes rather than technical features

or capabilities
- **Problem-Solution Framework**: Position yourself as someone who understands the pain points and has proven solutions
- **Peer-to-Peer Approach**: Speak as a fellow business owner rather than as a consultant or expert looking down

The most powerful positioning comes from understanding that your audience consists of people facing the same challenges you once faced. They need someone who speaks their language, understands their constraints, and has successfully navigated the path they're considering. Your role is to be their guide, not their guru.

Building Your Thought Leadership Platform

Thought leadership in the AI space requires a multi-channel approach that demonstrates your expertise while providing genuine value to your audience. The platform you build becomes the foundation for everything else—speaking opportunities, partnerships, consulting requests, and media coverage all flow from having established yourself as a credible voice in the AI conversation.

Content creation forms the backbone of your platform

Your AI implementation story provides rich material for multiple content formats. Blog posts detailing specific challenges and solutions, case studies showing before-and-after results, and video content walking through your process all help establish your expertise while providing value to others facing similar challenges.

The key is consistency and authenticity. Share regular updates about your ongoing AI journey, including new implementations, optimization results, and lessons learned. This ongoing documentation proves that your expertise is current and growing, not based on a single past success.

Speaking and presentation opportunities

Industry conferences, local business groups, and professional associations are always looking for speakers who can share practical, results-based insights. Your AI success story is exactly what these audiences want to hear—not theoretical possibilities, but real-world implementations with measurable outcomes.

Start with smaller, local opportunities to refine your message and build confidence. Chamber of Commerce meetings, industry meetups, and professional development sessions provide perfect venues for sharing your story and establishing your reputation as an AI leader.

Strategic networking and relationship building

Building relationships with other business leaders, industry influencers, and potential partners creates the network effect that amplifies your thought leadership. These relationships often lead to speaking opportunities, joint ventures, and referral partnerships that expand your influence and create new revenue streams.

Focus on providing value first in every interaction. Share insights, make introductions, and offer help without immediate expectation of return. This approach builds the trust and goodwill that forms the foundation of lasting professional relationships.

Creating Revenue Streams from Your AI Expertise

Your AI implementation success creates multiple opportunities for generating additional revenue streams that leverage your proven expertise. These opportunities often provide higher margins than your core business operations while requiring minimal additional infrastructure or overhead.

Consulting and advisory services represent the most direct monetization of your AI expertise. Other business owners facing AI implementation challenges will pay premium rates for guidance from someone who has successfully navigated the process. Your proven track record eliminates their risk and accelerates their timeline, making your services extremely valuable.

Structure your consulting to reflect the same systematic approach you used in your own implementation. This might include assessment services to identify AI opportunities, implementation planning and oversight, or ongoing optimization support. Each service level should be clearly defined with specific deliverables and outcomes.

Training and workshop delivery allows you to scale your expertise to multiple clients simultaneously. Develop workshops that teach other business owners your implementation methodology, share your lessons learned, and provide hands-on guidance for their specific situations.

These workshops can be delivered in multiple formats:
- Live, in-person sessions for local business groups

- Virtual workshops for broader geographic reach
- Self-paced online courses for passive income generation
- Corporate training for larger organizations

Strategic partnerships and joint ventures emerge naturally when you're recognized as an AI leader. Technology vendors want to partner with successful implementers, other service providers seek expertise to round out their offerings, and complementary businesses look for innovative partners who can enhance their value proposition.

These partnerships might include:
- Referral agreements with AI vendors
- Joint service offerings with complementary businesses
- Strategic alliances for larger project opportunities
- Advisory roles with technology companies

The Mentorship Multiplier Effect

Mentoring other business owners creates a multiplier effect that amplifies your influence while generating additional opportunities for business development. When you help others achieve AI success, you create a network of advocates who refer opportunities, share your content, and enhance your reputation within the industry.

Formal mentorship programs provide structured ways to share your expertise while building relationships with emerging leaders in your industry. These programs might be sponsored by industry associations, chambers of commerce, or business development organizations.

Peer advisory groups create ongoing relationships with other business leaders who can become sources of referrals, partnerships, and collaborative opportunities. Your AI expertise makes you a valuable member of these groups while your participation keeps you connected to market trends and opportunities.

Success story amplification happens naturally when your mentees achieve their own AI implementation success. Their wins become testimonials for your guidance, creating social proof that attracts additional mentorship opportunities and consulting requests.

The key to effective mentorship is maintaining the same systematic approach you used in your own implementation. Provide clear frameworks, specific guidance, and ongoing support rather than vague encouragement or theoretical advice.

Industry Influence and Recognition Strategies

Building industry influence requires consistent visibility combined with valuable contributions to industry conversations. This influence becomes a competitive advantage that opens doors, creates opportunities, and positions your business for accelerated growth.

Industry publication contributions establish your credibility while reaching your target audience through channels they already trust. Trade magazines, industry websites, and professional journals provide platforms for sharing your insights while building your reputation as a thought leader.

Focus on practical, actionable content that helps readers solve real problems. Share specific examples from your implementation experience, provide frameworks others can use, and offer insights that save time or money. This approach positions you as helpful rather than promotional.

Conference speaking and panel participation puts you in front of your ideal audience while positioning you alongside other recognized industry leaders. The association with established experts enhances your credibility while the speaking opportunity demonstrates your expertise to potential clients and partners.

Award and recognition programs provide third-party validation of your AI success while generating positive publicity for your business. Industry awards, innovation recognitions, and business excellence programs offer opportunities to showcase your achievements while building your reputation.

Apply for awards that specifically recognize innovation, technology adoption, or business transformation. Your AI implementation story provides compelling material for award applications while the recognition process often generates valuable publicity and networking opportunities.

Leveraging Success for Business Development

Your AI leadership position becomes a powerful business development tool that attracts high-quality prospects while commanding premium pricing. Clients who seek out AI leaders are typically less price-sensitive and more focused on results, creating opportunities for more profitable engagements.

Inbound lead generation occurs naturally when you're recognized as an AI leader. Potential clients find you through your content, speaking engagements, and industry recognition rather than through traditional sales and marketing efforts. These inbound leads are typically higher quality and more likely to convert than prospects reached through outbound efforts.

Premium positioning allows you to command higher prices for your core services because clients associate AI leadership with superior capabilities and results. Your proven track record with AI implementation suggests that you'll bring the same innovative thinking and execution excellence to other projects.

Strategic partnerships emerge when other businesses want to associate with recognized leaders. These partnerships might include referral relationships, joint venture opportunities, or strategic alliances that expand your market reach and service capabilities.

Building Your AI Innovation Ecosystem

As an industry leader, you have the opportunity to create an ecosystem of relationships, resources, and opportunities that continuously reinforce your position while generating ongoing business value. This ecosystem becomes a sustainable competitive advantage that's difficult for competitors to replicate.

Vendor relationships provide early access to new technologies, preferred pricing, and marketing support that enhances your capabilities while reducing costs. AI vendors value relationships with successful implementers because they provide case studies, testimonials, and referral opportunities.

Peer networks create opportunities for collaboration, knowledge sharing, and mutual support. Building relationships with other AI leaders in complementary industries provides access to insights, best practices, and partnership opportunities that accelerate your continued innovation.

Industry advisory roles position you as an influential voice in the direction of AI adoption within your industry. These roles might include advisory board positions with technology companies, committee participation with industry associations, or consultation opportunities with policy-making organizations.

Measuring and Communicating Your Leadership Impact

Documenting and communicating your impact as an AI leader reinforces your position while providing content for ongoing thought leadership efforts. The key is measuring both quantitative results and qualitative influence to tell a comprehensive story of your leadership journey.

Business impact metrics provide concrete evidence of how your AI leadership has translated into business results. Track metrics such as:

- Revenue increases from new service offerings
- Client acquisition through thought leadership activities
- Premium pricing achieved through positioning
- Partnership opportunities generated through industry relationships

Industry influence indicators measure your growing influence within your sector:

- Speaking invitations and conference participation
- Media mentions and industry publication features
- Advisory roles and committee appointments
- Peer recognition and award nominations

Community impact measures show how your leadership is helping others achieve AI success:

- Number of businesses mentored or advised
- Success stories from your guidance and support
- Industry adoption rates influenced by your advocacy
- Knowledge sharing through content and presentations

Future-Proofing Your Leadership Position

Maintaining your position as an AI leader requires continuous learning, innovation, and adaptation as the technology continues to advance rapidly. The strategies that establish your leadership must be balanced with ongoing efforts to stay current and relevant.

Continuous learning and development ensures your expertise remains current and valuable. This includes staying informed about new AI technologies, attending industry conferences, and participating in professional development opportunities that expand your knowledge and capabilities.

Innovation and experimentation demonstrate that your leadership is based on ongoing success rather than past achievements. Continue implementing new AI solutions, testing emerging technologies, and pushing the boundaries of what's possible in your industry.

Knowledge sharing and teaching reinforce your expertise while building relationships with the next generation of AI leaders. Your willingness to share knowledge demonstrates confidence in your capabilities while creating goodwill that supports your long-term influence.

Creating Your Leadership Legacy

The ultimate goal of becoming an AI leader isn't just personal recognition or short-term business gains—it's creating a lasting impact that transforms your industry while building sustainable competitive advantages for your business. Your leadership journey creates value that extends far beyond immediate financial returns.

When you successfully establish yourself as an AI leader, you create a legacy that includes the businesses you've helped transform, the industry standards you've influenced, and the innovations you've championed. This legacy becomes a source of ongoing opportunities, relationships, and influence that supports continued business growth and personal satisfaction.

Your transformation from struggling with AI implementation to leading industry adoption proves that success isn't about having the biggest budget or the most technical expertise—it's about taking action, learning from experience, and sharing your journey with others. The leadership position you build becomes a platform for creating even greater impact while achieving the business success you originally sought through AI implementation.

As you prepare to take your next steps in building industry leadership, remember that your journey isn't ending—it's entering its most exciting phase. With your proven track record, growing expertise, and expanding influence, you're positioned to shape the future of AI adoption in your industry while building the business success you've always envisioned.

The next chapter will explore how to scale your AI implementations beyond your first success, building on your leadership position to create systematic approaches for expanding AI throughout your organization and maximizing the compound benefits of your growing expertise.

Chapter Nineteen

The Effortless Growth Engine

AI-POWERED BUSINESSES GROW WHILE their owners sleep, play, and strategize instead of grinding endlessly. What seems impossible to traditional business owners becomes inevitable when you understand how intelligent automation creates self-perpetuating growth cycles that expand market reach without expanding workload. This isn't about working smarter instead of harder—it's about creating systems so intelligent they make the concept of "hard work" obsolete. The businesses that survive the next decade won't be those that work the hardest, but those that architect growth engines that operate independently of their founder's daily involvement.

The Growth Paradox That's Killing Small Businesses

Most entrepreneurs believe a fundamental lie about business growth: that success requires proportional increases in effort, stress, and personal involvement. You've probably experienced this yourself—every new customer means more emails, every expansion requires more oversight, every opportunity demands more of your time. This linear thinking creates what I call the **Growth Trap**, where business owners become prisoners of their own success.

Traditional business models operate on a simple but destructive premise: growth equals more work. Need to double revenue? Double your effort. Want to expand into new markets? Personally oversee every detail. This approach worked when businesses competed primarily on execution and customer service, but it's become a death sentence in the AI era.

The math is brutal and unforgiving. If your business requires your personal involvement to grow, you've built a sophisticated job, not a business. You're trading time for money at scale, which means you'll always hit a ceiling determined by the number of hours you can physically work. Meanwhile, AI-enhanced competitors are building systems that scale infinitely without human intervention.

Consider Christine, who owns a marketing consultancy. For three years, she grew from $200,000 to $800,000 in annual revenue by working longer days, hiring more staff, and personally managing every client relationship. But she hit a wall at $800,000 because growth required her to be involved in every decision, review every campaign, and handle every crisis. She was working 70-hour weeks and couldn't take a vacation without her phone constantly ringing.

Then Christine discovered AI-powered project management systems, automated client communication tools, and predictive analytics for campaign optimization. Within six months, her business grew to $1.2 million while she worked 30% fewer hours. The AI systems handled routine decisions, identified opportunities automatically, and optimized performance without her oversight. She had accidentally built an effortless growth engine.

Advanced AI Strategies for Automated Business Development

The most successful AI-enhanced businesses don't just use automation to handle existing processes—they use AI to identify, pursue, and close new opportunities without human intervention. This represents a fundamental shift from reactive business development to proactive opportunity hunting that never sleeps.

Intelligent Lead Generation Systems operate like having a team of researchers working 24/7 to identify perfect prospects. Modern AI tools can scan social media, industry publications, job postings, and company websites to identify businesses showing specific buying signals. For example, if you provide marketing services, AI can identify companies that just hired new marketing directors, launched new products, or posted job openings for marketing roles.

The system doesn't just find leads—it qualifies them based on your ideal customer profile, scores them by likelihood to convert, and even crafts personalized outreach messages based on their specific situation. While you sleep, your AI system is building relationships with prospects who are most likely to become profitable customers.

Automated Relationship Nurturing takes prospect development to the next level. Instead of sending generic email sequences, AI systems analyze prospect behavior, engagement patterns, and company developments to deliver perfectly timed, highly relevant content. The system knows when a prospect visits your pricing page, downloads a specific resource, or engages with your content on social media.

Based on these signals, the AI automatically adjusts the nurturing sequence, sends relevant case studies, or alerts your sales team when prospects show high-intent behaviors. It's like having a psychic sales assistant who knows exactly what each prospect needs to hear and when they need to hear it.

Predictive Opportunity Identification represents the cutting edge of automated business development. These systems analyze patterns in your existing customer base, market trends, and industry developments to predict where new opportunities will emerge before your competitors even recognize them.

For instance, an AI system might analyze patent filings, regulatory changes, and industry spending patterns to predict that companies in a specific sector will need your services in the next six months. It then proactively identifies and begins nurturing relationships with those companies before they even realize they have a need.

AI Business Development Strategy	Traditional Approach Time Investment	AI-Automated Time Investment	Effectiveness Multiplier
Lead Research & Qualification	20 hours/week	2 hours/week setup	5x more qualified leads
Prospect Nurturing	15 hours/week	1 hour/week monitoring	8x higher conversion rates
Opportunity Identification	10 hours/week	30 minutes/week review	12x more opportunities
Relationship Management	25 hours/week	3 hours/week oversight	4x stronger relationships

Scaling Operations Without Proportional Stress Increases

The secret to effortless growth lies in building operations that become more efficient as they scale, rather than more complex. Traditional businesses experience what economists call "diseconomies of scale"—the point where growth creates more problems than profits. AI-enhanced businesses create the opposite effect through intelligent automation that improves with volume.

Adaptive Workflow Management ensures that increased business volume doesn't translate to increased operational complexity. Instead of hiring more people to handle more work, AI systems automatically distribute tasks, optimize resource allocation, and identify bottlenecks before they impact performance.

When order volume doubles, the AI doesn't just process twice as many orders—it learns from the increased data to optimize routing, predict delivery times more accurately, and identify patterns that improve the entire fulfillment process. The system gets smarter and more efficient as it handles more volume.

Intelligent Quality Control maintains service standards regardless of scale. Traditional businesses struggle with quality consistency as they grow because human oversight becomes diluted across more activities. AI systems monitor quality indicators in real-time, automatically flagging issues, and implementing corrections before customers notice problems.

An AI system monitoring customer service interactions can identify when response times are increasing, sentiment scores are declining, or specific types of issues are becoming more common. It automatically adjusts staffing, provides real-time coaching to service representatives, and escalates critical issues to ensure quality remains consistent even during growth spurts.

Predictive Resource Planning eliminates the guesswork from scaling operations. Instead of reactive hiring and capacity planning, AI systems analyze business patterns, seasonal trends, and growth indicators to predict resource needs weeks or months in advance.

The system knows that based on current lead generation rates and historical conversion patterns, you'll need additional customer service capacity in eight weeks. It automatically initiates the hiring process, orders additional equipment, and adjusts workflow systems to accommodate the increased volume before you even realize you need it.

Self-Managing Customer Success Systems

Customer retention and expansion become automatic when AI systems monitor customer health, predict churn risk, and proactively intervene to ensure success. These systems don't just track customer satisfaction—they actively work to improve it through intelligent interventions and personalized experiences.

Behavioral Pattern Recognition identifies subtle signals that predict customer success or failure long before traditional metrics reveal problems. The AI analyzes login frequency, feature usage patterns, support ticket themes, and engagement levels to create early warning systems for customer health.

When a customer's usage pattern changes in ways that historically predict churn, the system automatically triggers personalized re-engagement campaigns, alerts the customer success team, or provides additional training resources. The customer receives help before they even realize they need it.

Automated Success Optimization continuously improves the customer experience through intelligent testing and personalization. The AI system runs constant experiments on email timing, content personalization, feature recommendations, and support approaches to optimize outcomes for each customer segment.

Instead of one-size-fits-all customer success programs, each customer receives a personalized experience optimized for their specific usage patterns, business goals, and communication preferences. The system learns what works for each type of customer and automatically applies those insights to similar customers.

Expansion Opportunity Detection identifies upselling and cross-selling opportunities based on customer behavior rather than arbitrary timelines. The AI analyzes usage patterns, business growth indicators, and feature requests to determine when customers are ready for additional products or services.

When a customer consistently hits usage limits, requests specific features, or shows patterns similar to customers who have successfully expanded their accounts, the system automatically provides relevant information, trial access, or personalized expansion proposals.

Creating Sustainable Competitive Advantages Through AI-First Business Models

The ultimate goal of the effortless growth engine is to create competitive advantages so significant that competitors can't replicate them without completely rebuilding their business models. This happens when AI integration becomes so deep that it fundamentally changes how value is created and delivered.

Data-Driven, Competitive Moats emerge when your AI systems have access to proprietary data sets that improve their performance in ways competitors can't match. As your systems process more customer interactions, transactions, and market data, they become increasingly intelligent and effective.

A recommendation engine gets better with more user data. A demand forecasting system becomes more accurate with more transaction history. A customer service AI becomes more helpful with more support interactions. Competitors starting from zero can't immediately replicate the intelligence your systems have developed through years of data processing.

Network Effect Amplification occurs when AI systems create value that increases with the number of participants in your ecosystem. Each new customer, partner, or data source makes the system more valuable for all existing participants.

Consider a logistics platform where AI optimizes delivery routes. Each new delivery driver provides more data points for route optimization. Each new customer adds more destinations that can be efficiently combined. Each new partner location creates additional optimization opportunities. The platform becomes exponentially more valuable as it grows, creating barriers to entry that increase over time.

Intelligent Market Positioning allows AI systems to automatically adjust pricing, messaging, and positioning based on competitive intelligence and market conditions. Instead of manual competitor monitoring and reactive strategy adjustments, AI systems continuously analyze competitive landscapes and optimize your positioning for maximum advantage.

The system monitors competitor pricing, messaging changes, customer feedback, and market trends to automatically adjust your strategy. When a competitor raises prices, your system might automatically adjust your positioning to emphasize value. When market conditions change, messaging automatically adapts to address new customer priorities.

The Compound Effect of AI-Enhanced Decision Making

Perhaps the most powerful aspect of effortless growth engines is their ability to make better decisions more quickly and consistently than human managers. Each decision improvement compounds over time, creating exponential advantages that become impossible for competitors to overcome.

Real-Time Market Adaptation allows businesses to respond to opportunities and threats faster than humanly possible. While competitors are scheduling meetings to discuss market changes, AI-enhanced businesses are already adjusting strategies and capturing opportunities.

When a new market trend emerges, AI systems can immediately analyze the implications, identify relevant opportunities, adjust marketing messages, reallocate resources, and implement tactical changes across the entire organization. What used to take weeks of analysis and planning happens in minutes.

Intelligent Resource Optimization ensures that every business resource is deployed for maximum impact. AI systems continuously analyze the performance of marketing campaigns, sales activities, operational processes, and strategic initiatives to optimize resource allocation in real-time.

Instead of quarterly planning cycles and annual budget reviews, optimization happens continuously. Underperforming campaigns are automatically paused. High-performing activities receive additional resources. Seasonal patterns trigger proactive adjustments. The business operates at peak efficiency without constant management oversight.

Predictive Strategic Planning uses AI analysis of market trends, customer behavior, and competitive intelligence to identify strategic opportunities and threats months before they become obvious to traditional analysis.

The system might predict that a specific customer segment will become more price-sensitive based on economic indicators, automatically adjusting pricing strategies and value propositions before competitors recognize the trend. Or it might identify an emerging market opportunity and begin preliminary positioning efforts while competitors are still focused on current markets.

Implementation Roadmap for Your Effortless Growth Engine

Building an effortless growth engine requires systematic implementation that builds capabilities progressively. Start with high-impact, low-complexity automation and gradually add sophisticated AI capabilities as your systems mature and your confidence grows.

Phase 1: Foundation Building (Weeks 1-4)

- Implement basic lead generation automation
- Set up customer behavior tracking systems
- Deploy automated email nurturing sequences
- Install predictive analytics for key business metrics

Phase 2: Intelligence Integration (Weeks 5-8)

- Add behavioral pattern recognition for customer success
- Implement automated opportunity identification
- Deploy intelligent workflow management
- Install real-time performance optimization

Phase 3: Advanced Automation (Weeks 9-12)

- Launch predictive resource planning systems
- Implement automated competitive intelligence
- Deploy adaptive pricing and positioning algorithms
- Install comprehensive business intelligence dashboards

Phase 4: Optimization and Scaling (Weeks 13-16)

- Fine-tune all automated systems based on performance data
- Implement advanced personalization engines
- Deploy predictive market analysis capabilities
- Launch intelligent expansion opportunity detection

The key to successful implementation is starting with systems that provide immediate value while building the data foundation needed for more sophisticated AI capabilities. Each phase builds upon previous capabilities, creating a growth engine that becomes more powerful and autonomous over time.

Your effortless growth engine won't happen overnight, but it will happen faster than you think if you start with the right foundation and follow a systematic implementation approach. The businesses that begin building these capabilities today will dominate their markets tomorrow, while competitors who wait for "perfect readiness" will find themselves permanently behind.

The transformation from manual business management to effortless growth isn't just about adopting new tools—it's about fundamentally reimagining what business ownership can look like when intelligence, rather than effort, drives results.

Your AI-Powered Future Starts Now

The moment you close this book marks the beginning of your AI advantage.

For the past several chapters, you've journeyed from fear-based hesitation to confident implementation readiness. You've learned that the Shadow Implementation Method isn't just another business strategy—it's your secret weapon for gaining competitive advantages while your rivals remain trapped in analysis paralysis. You've discovered that the SHADOW Framework provides the exact roadmap for implementing profitable AI solutions in 60 days without operational disruption.

The Complete Journey From AI Paralysis to AI Mastery

Remember where you started this journey. You picked up this book because AI felt overwhelming, risky, and impossibly complex. You watched competitors potentially gaining ground while you remained stuck in endless research cycles. The fear of making costly mistakes paralyzed you, and the technical jargon made AI feel like a foreign language spoken only by Silicon Valley insiders.

That version of you no longer exists.

Through this book, you've undergone a fundamental transformation. You've learned that AI implementation doesn't require technical expertise—it requires the right methodology. You've discovered that the businesses dominating tomorrow aren't the ones with the biggest budgets or the most technical knowledge. They're the ones bold enough to start before they feel completely ready.

Your transformation includes these critical mindset shifts:

- **From perfectionist to implementer**: You now understand that waiting for perfect readiness guarantees you'll miss the competitive window entirely
- **From researcher to action-taker**: You've learned that the AI revolution rewards those who learn while doing, not those who learn before doing
- **From fearful to confident**: The Shadow Implementation Method has shown you how to test AI solutions without risking operational disruption
- **From follower to leader**: You're now equipped to become the AI innovator in your industry while competitors remain stuck in planning mode

The psychological barriers that once held you back have been systematically dismantled. You've learned that implementation fears are normal but conquerable. You've discovered that technical helplessness is actually a myth perpetuated by those who benefit from your hesitation. Most importantly, you've realized that your business doesn't need to be "AI-ready" to start gaining AI advantages.

Your journey has been methodical and purposeful. Part I awakened you to the reality that early action beats perfect preparation. Part II equipped you with the complete SHADOW Framework for risk-free implementation. Part III showed you how to scale beyond your first success into comprehensive AI mastery.

This transformation positions you in an elite group of business owners who understand that competitive advantages come from strategic implementation, not endless preparation. You're no longer the business owner who watches from the sidelines while others innovate. You're the one who acts while others analyze.

Your Business Operating With AI-Powered Competitive Advantages

Close your eyes and envision your business six months from now. Your AI systems are humming quietly in the background, handling tasks that once consumed hours of your day. Customer inquiries are answered instantly with personalized responses that delight rather than frustrate. Your marketing campaigns target prospects with surgical precision, generating higher conversion rates than you've ever achieved.

Your operations run with clockwork efficiency. Inventory levels optimize themselves based on predictive analytics. Scheduling conflicts resolve automatically. Financial forecasts provide crystal-clear insights into future performance, allowing you to make decisions with confidence rather than guesswork.

Here's what your AI-powered competitive advantages look like in practice:

Customer Experience Excellence

Your customers receive service that feels impossibly personalized and responsive. AI systems anticipate their needs, recommend relevant products, and resolve issues before they become problems. While competitors struggle with generic customer service, you're delivering experiences that create raving fans and vocal advocates.

Operational Efficiency Mastery

Tasks that once required manual oversight now manage themselves. Your team focuses on high-value activities while AI handles the repetitive work that drains productivity. You're accomplishing more with the same resources, creating profit margins that give you flexibility your competitors lack.

Marketing Precision Targeting

Your marketing budget generates returns that seem almost unfair. AI-powered targeting identifies your ideal customers with accuracy that transforms advertising from expense to investment. You're reaching the right people with the right message at the right time, while competitors spray marketing dollars hoping something sticks.

Financial Intelligence Clarity

Your financial decisions are guided by AI insights that reveal patterns invisible to traditional analysis. Cash flow predictions help you avoid financial stress. Investment decisions are supported by data-driven projections rather than hopeful guessing. You're operating with the financial intelligence of a Fortune 500 company.

Innovation Leadership Position

Your industry views you as the forward-thinking innovator who "figured it out first." Customers seek you out because they know you're using cutting-edge solutions to serve them better. Competitors study your moves, trying to replicate advantages they don't understand.

This isn't fantasy—it's the predictable result of implementing the strategies in this book. The Shadow Implementation Method ensures you achieve these advantages without the operational risks that paralyze other business owners. You're not gambling with your business stability. You're systematically building competitive advantages through proven methodologies.

Your customers notice the difference immediately. They experience faster response times, more accurate information, and personalized service that exceeds their expectations. They start recommending your business to others, not just because of what you sell, but because of how brilliantly you serve them.

Your team operates with newfound efficiency and focus. They're freed from mind-numbing repetitive tasks and empowered to contribute in ways that genuinely matter. Morale improves because work becomes more engaging and meaningful. Productivity soars because AI handles the busy work while humans focus on creative problem-solving.

Your financial performance reflects these operational improvements. Profit margins improve because you're accomplishing more with the same resources. Revenue grows because you're serving customers better than competitors. Cash flow becomes more predictable because AI helps you anticipate and plan for future needs.

The Compound Effect of Early AI Adoption

Your early adoption creates advantages that multiply exponentially over time. While competitors remain stuck in research mode, you're gaining practical experience that translates into deeper competitive moats. Every month you operate with AI advantages is another month your competitors fall further behind.

Understanding the compound effect requires recognizing how early advantages snowball:

Experience Accumulation

Each day you operate AI systems, you gain insights that competitors lack. You learn what works, what doesn't, and how to optimize performance. This practical knowledge becomes intellectual property that can't be purchased or quickly replicated.

Data Network Effects

Your AI systems become smarter over time as they process more data from your operations. The recommendations become more accurate, the predictions more reliable, and the automation more sophisticated. Competitors starting later begin with inferior data sets and less refined algorithms.

Customer Relationship Deepening

Your AI-enhanced customer experiences create loyalty that competitors struggle to overcome. Customers become accustomed to your superior service levels and find competitor offerings frustratingly inadequate by comparison. Switching costs increase as customers integrate with your AI-powered solutions.

Operational Efficiency Compounding

The time and cost savings from AI implementation free up resources for additional innovations. You can invest in new AI applications while competitors are still implementing their first solutions. Your operational advantage compounds as you deploy AI across more business functions.

Market Position Strengthening

Your reputation as an AI innovator attracts customers, partners, and opportunities that might otherwise go to competitors. You become the obvious choice for customers who value innovation and efficiency. Your market position strengthens through association with cutting-edge solutions.

Consider the mathematical reality of compound advantages. If your AI implementations provide just a 10% efficiency improvement each quarter, you're operating at 146% of your original capacity after two years. Competitors who wait two years to start are facing a business that's nearly 50% more efficient than when they first considered AI adoption.

The timing advantages are particularly pronounced in rapidly changing markets. Early AI adopters establish market positions that become increasingly difficult to challenge. They build customer relationships based on superior service delivery. They develop operational capabilities that create cost structures competitors can't match.

Your early adoption also provides crucial learning time. You discover which AI applications provide the highest ROI for your specific business model. You develop internal expertise that becomes a strategic asset. You build confidence through small wins that prepare you for larger implementations.

This compound effect extends beyond your immediate business results. Your industry reputation evolves from follower to leader. Customers seek you out specifically because they know you're using advanced solutions. Media and industry publications highlight your innovations. Speaking opportunities position you as a thought leader.

The competitive moats you're building become deeper over time. New competitors entering your market face the daunting task of competing against AI-enhanced operations. Existing competitors struggle to match service levels you're delivering through automated systems. Your advantages compound while their disadvantages multiply.

Your Call-to-Action for Immediate Implementation

The time for preparation has ended—the time for implementation begins now. You have everything needed to start your AI transformation within the next 24 hours. The SHADOW Framework provides your roadmap. Your newfound confidence provides your motivation. The competitive window provides your urgency.

Here's your specific action plan for immediate implementation:

Today (Next 2 Hours)

1. **Complete your initial process audit**: Review your business operations using the screening criteria from Chapter 6. Identify three potential AI opportunities that meet the high-impact, low-risk criteria.

2. **Calculate preliminary ROI estimates**: Use the methods from Chapter 6 to estimate potential cost savings and revenue increases for each opportunity. Focus on applications with 3:1 ROI potential within 60 days.

3. **Select your golden opportunity**: Choose the single AI implementation that offers the highest probability of success combined with meaningful business impact.

This Week (Next 7 Days)

1. **Begin data collection**: Start gathering the historical data and performance metrics needed for your shadow implementation. Document current process performance to establish baseline measurements.

2. **Research AI vendors**: Identify 3-5 potential AI solutions that align with your selected opportunity. Focus on vendors offering trial periods and implementation support.

3. **Secure stakeholder buy-in**: Present your implementation plan to key team members and secure their support for the shadow implementation approach.

Weeks 2-3 (Days 8-21)

1. **Vendor evaluation and selection**: Complete vendor evaluations using the framework from Chapter 8. Negotiate trial periods and implementation support terms.

2. **Solution configuration**: Set up your chosen AI solution to mirror your existing process parameters. Ensure parallel operation capabilities without disrupting current workflows.

3. **Team preparation**: Train designated staff members to oversee the shadow system operations and monitoring protocols.

Weeks 4-7 (Days 22-49)

1. **Shadow deployment**: Launch your AI solution in parallel with existing operations. Monitor performance daily and compare results against baseline metrics.

2. **Performance optimization**: Analyze performance gaps and adjust AI parameters based on real-world results. Document improvements in speed, accuracy, and cost reduction.

3. **ROI documentation**: Create detailed reports demonstrating measurable business value and preparing for full integration decisions.

Weeks 8-9 (Days 50-63)

1. **Integration planning**: Develop your transition plan from shadow to full operational integration. Minimize disruption during the cutover period.

2. **Team training completion**: Ensure entire team is prepared for the AI-enhanced process and understands new protocols.

3. **Full implementation**: Complete the transition to full operational integration while maintaining monitoring systems for sustained performance.

Your success depends on starting immediately, not on perfect preparation. The competitive advantages outlined in this book only benefit those who implement them. Reading about the Shadow Implementation Method provides knowledge. Using the Shadow Implementation Method provides competitive advantages.

Remove every excuse that might delay your start:
- **"I need more research"**: You have sufficient knowledge to begin with a low-risk shadow implementation
- **"I need bigger budget"**: Start with high-ROI applications that pay for themselves within 60 days
- **"I need technical expertise"**: The Shadow Implementation Method specifically designed for non-technical business owners
- **"I need perfect timing"**: Competitive timing favors early action over perfect conditions

Your competitors are making these same excuses right now. While they research and analyze, you'll be implementing and optimizing. While they plan and prepare, you'll be gaining practical experience and competitive advantages. While they wait for certainty, you'll be creating the future of your industry.

The implementation process becomes easier once you start. The first step eliminates the paralysis. The first success builds confidence. The first competitive advantage creates momentum. Each subsequent implementation becomes faster and more effective because you're building on proven success patterns.

Final Reminder: The AI Revolution Rewards Early Action
The central truth of this book bears repeating one final time: The AI revolution rewards businesses that start before they're ready, not after they're certain. This principle separates the businesses that thrive in the AI era from those that struggle to catch up after missing the competitive window.

History validates this principle repeatedly. The businesses that dominated the internet age weren't the ones with perfect websites—they were the ones with websites first. The companies that captured mobile market share weren't those with flawless apps—they were those with apps earliest. The organizations winning the AI revolution won't be those with perfect implementations—they'll be those with implementations first.

Your window of opportunity is narrowing every day. Early AI adoption advantages are most pronounced when few competitors have implemented AI solutions. As more businesses adopt AI, the competitive advantage of early adoption diminishes. The businesses gaining advantages today will defend those advantages tomorrow.

The cost of waiting increases exponentially over time. Today's implementation gives you months or years of competitive advantage. Tomorrow's implementation puts you months or years behind early adopters. The difference between starting now and starting later isn't measured in implementation time—it's measured in competitive position.

Consider the businesses that will dominate your industry five years from now. They won't be the ones with the most resources or the most experience. They'll be the ones that implemented AI solutions while their competitors researched AI possibilities. They'll be the ones that gained practical experience while others gained theoretical knowledge.

Your choice is binary: lead or follow. Leading means starting your AI implementation immediately using the Shadow Implementation Method. Following means watching others implement AI solutions while you prepare for implementation. Leading means gaining competitive advantages while others analyze competitive threats.

The uncertainty that paralyzes other business owners should energize you. Uncertainty creates opportunity for those bold enough to act. The businesses that thrive during uncertain times are those that turn uncertainty into competitive advantage through strategic action.

Your competitive advantage isn't just the AI solutions you implement—it's your willingness to implement them before feeling completely ready. This psychological advantage compounds over time as you become comfortable with strategic risk-taking while competitors remain paralyzed by perfectionist thinking.

The Shadow Implementation Method gives you the perfect tool for maintaining this competitive advantage. You can continue testing new AI solutions while competitors struggle with their first implementations. You can iterate and improve while they plan and prepare. You can scale AI across your operations while they scale their research efforts.

Remember the transformation you've experienced through this book. You started with AI paralysis and finish with AI confidence. You began with implementation fears and conclude with implementation frameworks. You entered as a follower and emerge as a leader ready to shape your industry's future.

The AI revolution isn't coming—it's here. The question isn't whether AI will transform your industry—it's whether you'll lead that transformation or react to it. The businesses writing the future of your industry are the ones implementing AI solutions today, not the ones planning to implement AI solutions someday.

Your AI-powered future starts the moment you decide to start. The Shadow Implementation Method removes the risks. The SHADOW Framework provides the roadmap. Your newfound confidence supplies the motivation. The only thing missing is your decision to begin.

Close this book, open your laptop, and start your process audit today. Your competitors are still reading about AI implementation while you begin AI implementation. Your industry leadership journey begins with your first shadow deployment. Your competitive advantage starts with your first action.

The AI revolution rewards those who start before they're ready. You're ready to start. Your time to lead begins now.

As you step into your role as an AI implementation leader, remember that every successful transformation begins with a single decision followed by immediate action. Your industry is waiting for someone to show them what AI-powered success looks like. That someone is you. Your AI awakening starts now.

APPENDICES

RIVANNA HEIGHTS MEDIA

Appendix A: SHADOW Framework Implementation Checklist

THE DIFFERENCE BETWEEN SUCCESSFUL AI implementations and failed attempts often comes down to a single overlooked detail. This comprehensive checklist ensures you execute every critical step of the SHADOW Framework with precision and accountability.

Screen Phase Checklist

Process Audit and Opportunity Identification

[ ] Document all current business processes (minimum 10 core workflows)

[ ] Time each process from start to finish (3 measurement cycles minimum)

[ ] Identify bottlenecks and inefficiencies in each workflow

[ ] Calculate current labor costs for each process (hourly rate × time required)

[ ] Rank processes by time consumption (highest to lowest impact)

[ ] Assess technical complexity of each process (1-5 scale)

[ ] Evaluate data availability for each potential AI opportunity

[ ] Score processes using the Impact vs. Complexity matrix

ROI Calculation and Opportunity Selection

[ ] Calculate potential time savings for top 3 opportunities (hours per week)

[ ] Estimate cost reduction potential (labor + efficiency gains)

[ ] Project revenue increase possibilities (faster processing, better quality)

[ ] Research average AI solution costs for your selected opportunity

[ ] Calculate break-even timeline for each opportunity

[ ] Select opportunity with 3:1 ROI potential within 60 days

[ ] Document selection rationale for stakeholder presentation

[ ] Set specific, measurable success criteria

Harvest Phase Checklist

Data Collection and Preparation

[ ] Identify all data sources relevant to your selected opportunity

[ ] Assess data quality and completeness (accuracy percentage)

[ ] Clean and organize historical data (minimum 6 months recommended)

[ ] Export data in compatible formats (CSV, Excel, JSON)

[ ] Create data backup systems and security protocols

[ ] Document data collection processes for team training

[ ] Establish ongoing data gathering procedures

[ ] Test data access and retrieval systems

Stakeholder Alignment and Resource Securing

[ ] Present business case to key stakeholders

[ ] Secure budget approval for AI implementation

[ ] Identify internal project champion

[ ] Define roles and responsibilities for implementation team

[ ] Schedule regular check-in meetings and progress reviews

[ ] Communicate implementation timeline to affected departments

[ ] Address concerns and resistance from team members

[ ] Establish success celebration and recognition plans

Acquire Phase Checklist

Vendor Research and Evaluation

[ ] Research 5-7 potential AI vendors using evaluation template

[ ] Request demos from top 3 vendor candidates

[ ] Compare pricing structures and hidden costs

[ ] Evaluate integration capabilities with existing systems

[ ] Assess vendor support quality and response times

[ ] Check references and case studies from similar businesses

[ ] Review contract terms and cancellation policies

[ ] Negotiate trial periods and implementation support

Solution Configuration and Setup

[ ] Complete vendor onboarding and account setup

[ ] Configure AI solution to match your process parameters

[ ] Set up user accounts and access permissions

[ ] Integrate with existing business systems (if applicable)

[ ] Test basic functionality and data flow

[ ] Customize settings for your specific business needs

[ ] Document configuration choices for future reference

[ ] Create backup and recovery procedures

Deploy Phase Checklist

Shadow System Launch

[ ] Launch AI solution in parallel with existing process

[ ] Monitor both systems simultaneously for 30 days minimum

[ ] Track performance metrics daily (speed, accuracy, cost)

[ ] Document any issues or unexpected behaviors

[ ] Compare AI output quality against existing process results

[ ] Measure time savings and efficiency improvements

[ ] Collect feedback from team members using both systems

[ ] Adjust parameters based on real-world performance

Performance Monitoring and Data Collection

[ ] Set up automated performance tracking dashboards

[ ] Create daily, weekly, and monthly reporting schedules

[ ] Monitor system uptime and reliability statistics

[ ] Track user adoption and engagement metrics

[ ] Document cost savings and revenue improvements

[ ] Identify areas for optimization and fine-tuning

[ ] Prepare interim reports for stakeholder updates

[ ] Maintain detailed logs for decision-making support

Optimize Phase Checklist

Performance Analysis and Improvement

[ ] Analyze 30 days of parallel operation data

[ ] Identify performance gaps and improvement opportunities

[ ] Fine-tune AI parameters for optimal results

[ ] Test different configuration settings and approaches

[ ] Measure impact of optimization changes

[ ] Document best practices and lessons learned

[ ] Create performance benchmarks for ongoing monitoring

[ ] Prepare comprehensive ROI analysis report

Value Documentation and Business Case Creation

[ ] Calculate total time savings achieved (hours per week/month)

[ ] Document cost reductions and efficiency improvements

[ ] Measure quality improvements and error reduction

[ ] Quantify revenue increases or opportunity creation

[ ] Create visual reports and dashboards for stakeholders

[ ] Prepare case study documentation for future implementations

[ ] Calculate actual ROI against initial projections

[ ] Document unexpected benefits and discoveries

Weave Phase Checklist

Integration Planning and Execution

[ ] Develop detailed transition plan from shadow to full operation

[ ] Schedule integration timeline with minimal business disruption

[ ] Create backup plans for potential integration challenges

[ ] Train entire team on new AI-enhanced process

[ ] Update standard operating procedures and documentation

[ ] Establish new workflows and approval processes

[ ] Test full integration with small pilot group first

[ ] Execute complete transition to AI-powered operation

Ongoing Monitoring and Continuous Improvement

[ ] Implement permanent monitoring and reporting systems

[ ] Schedule regular performance reviews and optimization cycles

[ ] Create feedback collection mechanisms from team and customers

[ ] Establish escalation procedures for issues or problems

[ ] Plan for software updates and system maintenance

[ ] Document ongoing costs and ROI tracking methods

[ ] Identify opportunities for additional AI implementations

[ ] Celebrate success and recognize team contributions

Appendix B: Glossary of AI Terms for Small Business Owners

Understanding AI terminology is essential for confident vendor conversations and successful implementation decisions. This glossary translates technical jargon into practical business language.

Core AI Concepts

Artificial Intelligence (AI) Computer systems that perform tasks typically requiring human intelligence, such as pattern recognition, decision-making, and problem-solving. For small businesses, AI usually means software that automates processes, analyzes data, or improves customer interactions without constant human supervision.

Machine Learning (ML) A subset of AI where computer systems automatically improve their performance through experience without being explicitly programmed for each task. Think of it as software that gets smarter the more data it processes, like an email system that gets better at identifying spam over time.

Algorithm A set of rules or instructions that tells AI software how to solve problems or make decisions. Like a recipe for cooking, an algorithm provides step-by-step instructions for processing information and producing results.

Automation The use of technology to perform tasks with minimal human intervention. In business contexts, automation might handle data entry, customer communications, scheduling, or inventory management without requiring staff to manually complete each step.

Data Mining The process of analyzing large amounts of business data to discover patterns, trends, and insights that weren't obvious before. It's like having a super-powered detective that can spot hidden connections in your customer behavior, sales patterns, or operational efficiency.

Implementation and Integration Terms

API (Application Programming Interface) A connection method that allows different software systems to communicate and share data. Think of APIs as translators that help your existing business software talk to new AI tools without requiring complete system replacement.

Cloud Computing Accessing computer services (storage, software, processing power) over the internet instead of running everything on your own computers. Cloud-based AI solutions typically offer lower upfront costs and easier maintenance than installing software on your own servers.

Integration The process of connecting new AI software with your existing business systems so they work together seamlessly. Good integration means data flows automatically between systems without manual copying or duplicate data entry.

Deployment The process of putting AI software into active use in your business operations. Deployment can be done gradually (parallel with existing systems) or all at once (complete replacement of old processes).

Scalability The ability of an AI system to handle increasing amounts of work or users without major changes or performance problems. Scalable solutions grow with your business without requiring complete replacement.

Data and Analytics Terms

Big Data Large amounts of business information that would be difficult or impossible to analyze using traditional methods. For small businesses, "big data" might mean analyzing years of customer transactions, website interactions, or operational records to find improvement opportunities.

Analytics The systematic analysis of business data to discover meaningful patterns and support decision-making. Analytics turns raw numbers into actionable insights about customer behavior, business performance, or market trends.

Predictive Analytics Using historical data and AI to forecast future trends, behaviors, or outcomes. Examples include predicting which customers are likely to make purchases, when equipment might need maintenance, or what inventory levels you'll need next month.

Dashboard A visual display that shows key business metrics and AI insights in real-time, usually through charts, graphs, and summary numbers. Dashboards provide at-a-glance understanding of how your AI implementations are performing.

Data Quality A measure of how accurate, complete, and useful your business data is for AI analysis. High-quality data leads to better AI results, while poor data quality can cause AI systems to make incorrect predictions or recommendations.

Business Application Terms

Customer Relationship Management (CRM) AI AI features that enhance customer database software to predict customer needs, automate communications, and identify sales opportunities. CRM AI might suggest which customers to contact, when to follow up, or what products to recommend.

Chatbot AI software that can have text or voice conversations with customers, answering questions, providing information, or helping with simple tasks. Modern chatbots can handle many customer service interactions without human intervention.

Personalization Using AI to customize experiences, recommendations, or communications based on individual customer preferences and behavior patterns. Personalization makes each customer feel like you understand their specific needs and preferences.

Process Automation Using AI to handle routine business tasks automatically, such as data entry, report generation, appointment scheduling, or invoice processing. Process automation frees up staff time for higher-value activities.

Natural Language Processing (NLP) AI's ability to understand and respond to human language in text or speech. NLP powers chatbots, voice assistants, email analysis, and document processing systems.

Technical and Security Terms

Training Data The historical information used to teach AI systems how to perform specific tasks. Training data quality directly impacts AI performance—better historical data leads to more accurate AI predictions and recommendations.

Model The "brain" of an AI system that has been trained to perform specific tasks. Like a skilled employee, a well-trained model can handle similar situations consistently and accurately.

Accuracy Rate The percentage of time an AI system makes correct predictions or decisions. A 95% accuracy rate means the AI is correct 95 times out of 100, which might be better than human performance for specific tasks.

Latency The time delay between asking an AI system to perform a task and receiving the result. Low latency means fast response times, which is important for customer-facing applications.

Data Security Protecting business information from unauthorized access, theft, or misuse when using AI systems. This includes encryption, access controls, and compliance with privacy regulations.

Vendor and Service Terms

Software as a Service (SaaS) AI software that you access through the internet rather than installing on your own computers. SaaS solutions typically involve monthly or annual subscription fees and include maintenance and updates.

On-Premises AI software installed and running on your own computers or servers rather than in the cloud. On-premises solutions often require higher upfront costs but may offer more control over data and customization.

Implementation Support Services provided by AI vendors to help you set up, configure, and begin using their software successfully. Good implementation support can significantly reduce the time and effort required to start seeing benefits.

Service Level Agreement (SLA) A contract that specifies the performance standards and support commitments an AI vendor promises to deliver. SLAs typically cover system uptime, response times, and support availability.

Total Cost of Ownership (TCO) The complete cost of implementing and using an AI solution over time, including software fees, implementation services, training, support, and internal staff time. TCO provides a more accurate picture of true investment requirements than just software licensing costs.

Return on Investment Terms

Efficiency Gains Improvements in how quickly or effectively business processes are completed using AI. Efficiency gains might include faster processing times, reduced errors, or the ability to handle more work with the same staff.

Cost Savings Reductions in business expenses achieved through AI implementation, such as lower labor costs, reduced errors, decreased processing time, or eliminated manual tasks.

Revenue Enhancement Increases in business income enabled by AI capabilities, such as better customer service leading to more sales, faster processing allowing more transactions, or new AI-powered services you can offer customers.

Payback Period The amount of time required for the benefits of an AI investment to equal the total cost of implementation. A 12-month payback period means the cost savings and revenue increases will equal your AI investment within one year.

This comprehensive toolkit gives you everything needed to move from AI understanding to AI implementation with confidence. The checklists ensure nothing falls through the cracks, the vendor evaluation framework eliminates guesswork from selection decisions, the ROI worksheets provide compelling financial justification, and the glossary empowers you to navigate technical conversations with confidence.

Your next step is choosing which business process will become your first AI success story and beginning the SHADOW Framework implementation that transforms your business from AI-curious to AI-dominant.

References

10minmba. (n.d.). Network effects (The hidden engine behind billion-dollar empires). *10min MBA Newsletter*. https://newsletter.10minmba.com/p/network-effects-the-hidden-engine

Abmatic AI. (n.d.). Segmenting customers by behavior: Tips and best practices. https://abmatic.ai/blog/segmenting-customers-by-behavior-tips-and-best-practices

AI Agency Plus. (n.d.). Robotic process automation. https://aiagencyplus.com/robotic-process-automation/

AI-First Mindset. (n.d.). Human-AI collaboration: Boost your business productivity. https://aifirstmindset.ai/blog/human-ai-collaboration/

Airship. (n.d.). Customer experience automation explained. https://www.airship.com/resources/explainer/customer-experience-automation-explained/

AntSquad. (n.d.). Top SEO trends and strategies for 2025. https://antsquad.in/top-seo-trends-and-strategies-for-2025/

Attabotics. (n.d.). In a world of reduced spending - How to make automation make sense. https://attabotics.com/resource-center/in-a-world-of-reduced-spending-how-to-make-automation-make-sense/

Capturify. (2025). 7 best B2B email list building tools in 2025. https://www.capturify.io/blog-posts/b2b-email-list-building

DrChrono. (2024, November). How to transition to a new EHR system without losing data or productivity. *DrChrono Blog*. https://drchrono.com/blog/2024/11/how-to-transition-to-a-new-ehr-system-without-losing-data-or-productivity/

eReleases. (n.d.). What are the best ways to improve your company image? https://www.ereleases.com/pr-fuel/what-are-the-best-ways-to-improve-your-company-image/

Evans, H. (n.d.). 6 companies making AI more accessible. *Harmony Evans*. https://harmonyevans.com/6-companies-making-ai-more-accessible/

GetSuper AI. (n.d.). How Staples perform customer segmentation analysis to improve customer churn and retention. https://www.getsuper.ai/post/how-staples-perform-customer-segmentation-analysis-to-improve-customer-churn-and-retention

Haapala, N. (2024). *Evaluating low-code platforms for integration development: Benefits, challenges, and practical applications*. CORE. https://core.ac.uk/download/642686556.pdf

HighPerformr. (n.d.). 5 best practices for using social media scheduling tools. https://www.highperformr.ai/blog/best-practices-for-using-social-media-scheduling-tools

Inline Help. (n.d.). Chatbot development tools. https://inlinehelp.com/glossary/chatbot-development-tools/

INK. (n.d.). A quick guide for setting better employee goals. https://inkforall.com/hey-ink-tool/write-performance-review/employee-performance-goals-template/

KamilCoach. (n.d.). Professional productivity coaching. https://www.kamilcoach.com/process

Leeds Journal. (n.d.). Strategies to make yourself irresistible to investors. https://leedsjournal.co.uk/strategies-to-make-yourself-irresistible-to-investors/

Ntirety. (n.d.). Data modernization. https://www.ntirety.com/data/data-modernization/

OttoQA. (n.d.). Guide to preparing your contact center for AI integration. https://www.ottoqa.com/otto-blog/guide-to-preparing-your-contact-center-for-ai-integration

Rakuten India. (n.d.). Using AI for DevOps & operational efficiency - Rakuten India. https://corp.rakuten.co.in/rakathon-2024-blog-using-ai-for-devops-operational-efficiency/

Ravenswood Publishing. (n.d.). How data HK can help your business. https://ravenswoodpublishing.com/gambling-blog/how-data-hk-can-help-your-business/

rinf.tech. (n.d.). How AI turns data black holes into actionable insights in supply chain. https://www.rinf.tech/how-ai-turns-data-black-holes-into-actionable-insights-in-supply-chain/

RISE Marketing Group. (n.d.). Boosting customer retention: Mapping out the customer journey. https://risemarketinggroup.net/customer-journey-retention-strategies/

Superior Rio Web. (n.d.). Protecting your data: Accounting software security measures. https://superrioweb.com/28047-protecting-your-data-accounting-software-security-measures-47/

TaRanker. (2025). Shopify marketing and conversion apps 2025. https://taranker.com/shopify-marketing-and-conversion-apps

Techsaaz. (n.d.). 11 transformative AI applications reshaping small business operations. https://techsaaz.com/transformative-ai-applications/

Tendo. (n.d.). How do I become more productive? https://www.tendo-uk.com/how-do-i-become-more-productive/

The Business Concept. (n.d.). How to streamline financial tasks and reclaim your work-life balance. https://www.thebusinessconcept.com/how-to-streamline-financial-tasks-and-reclaim-your-work-life-balance/

Xpertz Out Source. (2025, February 6). Transforming business operations with AI-powered data and analytics. https://xpertzoutsource.com/2025/02/06/transforming-business-operations-with-ai-powered-data-and-analytics/

www.ingramcontent.com/pod-product-compliance
Lightning Source LLC
LaVergne TN
LVHW090356210926
848480LV00002B/356